WYNDHAM LEWIS PORTRAITS

PAUL EDWARDS

WITH RICHARD HUMPHREYS

NATIONAL PORTRAIT GALLERY, LONDON

WYNDHAM LEWIS PORTRAITS

ACKNOWLEDGEMENTS

I am grateful to Bath Spa University
for research leave, and to the Arts
and Humanities Research Council
for the award of a Knowledge Transfer
Fellowship for work on the exhibition.

In writing the catalogue, the works listed
in the Further Reading section have been
helpful; in particular, I am everywhere
indebted to the work of Jeffrey Meyers
and Paul O'Keeffe for their biographical
research. The Chronology could not have
been compiled without their work; the
reader is referred to the fuller chronology
in Meyers, 1980, pp.333–42.

Unless otherwise marked, all works
illustrated are by Wyndham Lewis
(1882–1957), and these, together with
all quotations from Lewis's writings
in the text, are copyright The Estate
of Mrs G.A. Wyndham Lewis. By
permission of the Wyndham Lewis
Memorial Trust (a registered charity)
unless otherwise stated.

Paul Edwards
Professor of English and History
of Art at Bath Spa University

Published in Great Britain by
National Portrait Gallery Publications,
National Portrait Gallery,
St Martin's Place, London WC2H 0HE

Published to accompany the exhibition
Wyndham Lewis Portraits at the
National Portrait Gallery, London
(3 July–19 October 2008).

For a complete catalogue of current
publications, please write to the
National Portrait Gallery at the
address above, or visit our website
www.npg.org.uk/publications

ISBN: 9781855143951

A catalogue record for this book is
available from the British Library.

Publishing Manager: Celia Joicey
Project Editor: Rebeka Cohen
Production: Ruth Müller-Wirth
and Geoff Barlow
Design: NB: Studio
Printed in Italy

Front cover: *T.S. Eliot*, 1938 (detail)
Durban Municipal Art Gallery (p.69)

Wyndham Lewis Portraits has
been supported by

 Arts & Humanities
Research Council

CONTENTS

WYNDHAM LEWIS WAS A MAN OF STRONG VIEWS, COMPLEX POLITICS AND VOLATILE FRIENDSHIPS; REFERRED TO BY W.H. AUDEN AS

'THAT LONELY OLD VOLCANO OF THE RIGHT'

FOREWORD

Wyndham Lewis was a man of strong views, complex politics and volatile friendships; referred to by W.H. Auden as 'that lonely old volcano of the Right'. Although arguably under-recognized in his lifetime, he was one of the most important figures in 20th-century British art. Alongside his work as a modernist activist, avant-garde artist, essayist and novelist, for which he was best known, he consistently made portraits. Before the First World War, through his period of work in North America, and at the end of his life back in London, the human subject engaged him again and again. He completed a number of telling commissioned portraits, and captured tenderly his wife Froanna, but Lewis was at his most powerful with his artistic peers: great writers and artists of the early and mid-20th century. The portraits of James Joyce, Edith Sitwell, Ezra Pound, Rebecca West, T.S. Eliot and Naomi Mitchison bristle with all the energy and charisma of maker and subject combined.

There is nothing half-hearted about Wyndham Lewis's works. Whether drawn or painted, his portraits are immediate and forthright. Paul Edwards and Richard Humphreys argue in their introduction that the apparent contradiction between his abstract work and the closely observed portraits can be resolved. Firstly, what is considered to be modern should be very much broader and not simply related to abstract form. And, secondly, they see it as a mark of the particular resonance of Lewis's portraits that there is an element of abstraction embedded within each work. As Lewis himself put it, 'burying Euclid deep in the living flesh'.

This book and the exhibition that it accompanies explore how portraiture and biography inform each other. They bring together works that have not been seen in Britain for many years, and in some cases have never been exhibited together. The National Portrait Gallery is therefore most grateful to both private and institutional lenders for their generosity in allowing precious works to be away on loan and to be illustrated here.

I should like to extend warm thanks to Paul Edwards, leading scholar on Wyndham Lewis and Professor of English and History of Art at Bath Spa University, and Richard Humphreys, curator and writer at Tate, for having instigated the exhibition and worked on the specific proposal for the Gallery. They have selected the works and led the project with the able support of Rebeka Cohen, Rosie Wilson and Paul Moorhouse to whom I am also grateful. I should also like to thank Pim Baxter, Denise Ellitson, Neil Evans, Susie Holden, Michelle Greaves, Sumi Ghose, Celia Joicey, Ruth Müller-Wirth, Jonathan Rowbotham, Liz Smith, Sarah Tinsley and Catherine Yexley, and all the National Portrait Gallery staff who have made the exhibition and this publication possible.

The Gallery gratefully acknowledges the generous support of the Arts and Humanities Research Council, The Wyndham Lewis Memorial Trust, The Old Possum's Practical Trust, Christie's, Hilary Newiss and Peter Bazalgette. Such help makes a real difference to the exhibition, the associated research and this publication.

Sandy Nairne
Director
National Portrait Gallery

CHRONOLOGY

1882
Percy Wyndham Lewis is born on 18 November in Amherst, Nova Scotia.

1897–8
Attends Rugby School in England.

1898–1901
Studies and is expelled from the Slade School of Fine Art, London.

1904–6
Meets Ida Vendel in Paris (Bertha in *Tarr*).

1906–7
Visits Munich; moves back to Paris; ends relationship with Ida.

1908–11
Writes a first draft of *Tarr*, a satirical depiction of bohemian life in Paris.

1909
First published writing, 'The "Pole"', appears in *The English Review*.

1911
Becomes a member of the Camden Town Group and produces cubist self-portrait drawings (p.21).

1912
Decorates the 'Cave of the Golden Calf' nightclub, London, and exhibits cubist paintings and illustrations to *Timon of Athens* at the *Second Post-Impressionist Exhibition*, London.

1913
Joins Roger Fry's Omega Workshops; walks out in October with Frederick Etchells, Edward Wadsworth (p.39) and Cuthbert Hamilton after quarrelling with Fry. The portfolio *Timon of Athens* is published, and Lewis begins a close artistic association with Ezra Pound (p.56; p.57; p.59; p.61; p.63).

1914
Becomes Director of the 'Rebel Art Centre' in London; disassociates himself from Futurism and disrupts a lecture by Marinetti at the Doré Gallery, London; Vorticism is officially launched in *Blast*, edited by Lewis; Lewis is introduced to T.S. Eliot by Pound (p.67; p.69; p.70; p.105; p.107).

1915
Contracts a venereal infection; *Blast*, no. 2, is published and *Tarr* is completed.

1916–18
War service in Royal Garrison Artillery, participating in the Third Battle of Ypres and working as Official War Artist for Canada and Great Britain.

1918–21
Lives with Iris Barry (p.35; p.36; p.37), with whom he has two children.

1918
Tarr is published. It is praised in reviews by Pound, Eliot and Rebecca West (p.79); meets future wife, Gladys Hoskins (p.93; p.95; p.96; p.97; p.98).

1919
One-man show (*Guns*) of war paintings and drawings. *Fifteen Drawings* is published, as is *The Caliph's Design: Architects! Where is Your Vortex?*, a pamphlet urging the continuance of modernism in art and its spread to architecture and town-planning.

1920
Forms Group X in an attempt to restore the avant-garde momentum of Vorticism in opposition to Bloomsbury conservatism; holidays in France with Eliot; meets James Joyce (p.64; p.65; p.66).

1921
Edits *The Tyro*, no. 1, a 'review of art and literature'; holds the *Tyros and Portraits* exhibition at Leicester Galleries, London (p.23; p.25; p.26); enjoys drinking sessions with Joyce in Paris.

1922
Lewis edits *The Tyro*, no. 2, containing a major aesthetic statement, 'Essay on the Objective of Plastic Art in our Time'; commissioned to produce a portrait of Edwin Evans (p.47); has an affair with Nancy Cunard (p.49); visits Venice with Cunard and the Sitwells (p.41; p.42; p.43; p.44; p.52); starts work on a portrait of Violet Schiff (p.51).

1923–4
Is given a monthly fund from Edward and Fanny Wadsworth, O.R. Drey and Richard Wyndham – all of whom Lewis later satirized in *The Apes of God*.

1925
Unsuccessfully submits a '500,000 word book', *The Man of the World*, to publishers; this is split up, revised and extended into separate books.

1926
Publishes *The Art of Being Ruled*, a work of political theory and analysis that attempts to distinguish sources of revolutionary change in society.

1927
Launches a new magazine, *The Enemy*, no. 1, which is largely written by Lewis and contains critiques of the literary avant-garde (including Pound and Joyce) for the political and philosophical naivety of their work; publishes *Time and Western Man* (which reprints essays from *The Enemy* and extends its critique to cover contemporary metaphysical theory); *The Enemy*, no. 2, is published (on the cult of the 'primitive' in the work of D.H. Lawrence and Sherwood Anderson); also publishes *The Lion and the Fox* (a study of Shakespeare) and *The Wild Body* (revisions of early short stories set in Brittany and Spain).

1928
A revised version of *Tarr* is published, as is *The Childermass: Section 1*, a fantasy of posthumous existence 'outside Heaven'.

1929
Publishes *Paleface: The Philosophy of the Melting Pot* (which reprints and extends essays published in *The Enemy*, no. 2) and *The Enemy*, no. 3 (a critique of the Parisian avant-garde); meets W.H. Auden and Stephen Spender (p.85).

CHRONOLOGY

1930
The Apes of God is published in a limited, signed edition: a satirical novel depicting the London art world of the 1920s; meets Naomi Mitchison (p.80; p.81; p.83); marries Gladys Hoskins (Froanna).

1931
Compiles *Hitler* from articles written for *Time and Tide* following a visit to Berlin; argues that Hitler is a 'man of peace'; visits Morocco.

1932
Lefevre Gallery (London) exhibition *Thirty Personalities and a Self Portrait*; publishes *Snooty Baronet*, a comic novel satirizing behaviourism (banned by Smiths and Boots lending libraries), *Filibusters in Barbary* (a travel book based on his experiences in Morocco) and *Doom of Youth* (a study of 'youth-politics'); both publications are suppressed after libel actions.

1933
Resumes painting in oils after a decade-long break; publishes *One-Way Song*, a book of poems.

1934
Men Without Art is published with critiques of Eliot, Virginia Woolf (p.45), William Faulkner and Ernest Hemingway.

1935
Collaborates with Mitchison on the illustrated fantasy *Beyond This Limit*.

1936
Publishes *Left Wings over Europe*, an anti-war book; paints *The Surrender of Barcelona* (now in Tate, London).

1937
Publishes *The Revenge for Love* (a tragic novel concerning deluded political commitments of the fashionable left-wing in the run-up to the Spanish Civil War), *Count your Dead: They are Alive!* (an anti-war book about the Spanish Civil War, sympathetic to the fascist side) and *Blasting and Bombardiering* (an autobiography); exhibition of drawings and paintings on metaphysical, historical and other themes at the Leicester Galleries; visits Berlin and Warsaw; declares he has been 'much deceived in politicians' in the special 'Wyndham Lewis's issue of *Twentieth Century Verse* (edited by Julian Symons) (p.88).

1938
Lewis's painting of Eliot is rejected by the Royal Academy in London; donates a painting for auction in aid of republican Spain; publishes *The Mysterious Mr. Bull* (a study of British character, praised by George Orwell: 'I do not think it is unfair to say that Mr. Wyndham Lewis has "gone left".'); begins a portrait of Pound (p.63).

1939
Attacks anti-semitism in *The Jews: Are they Human?*; collects writings on art in *Wyndham Lewis the Artist*, including a new essay advocating a return to nature (though not to naturalism); Lewis and Froanna leave for North America, spending three months in Buffalo, New York; paints Chancellor Samuel Capen (p.102); publishes *The Hitler Cult*.

1940
While based in Sag Harbor, Lewis finishes *The Vulgar Streak* (a novel set in 1938 at the time of the Munich Agreement which criticizes English class prejudice); moves to Toronto.

1941–2
Paints a series of watercolours exploring themes of creation, crucifixion and gestation; also a series of bathing scenes.

1941
The entire stock of an illustrated essay, 'The Role of Line in Art', published by patron Lord Carlow (p.87), is destroyed in a London air raid; Lewis notices a severe deterioration in his eyesight.

1945
Lewis and Froanna return to England with financial assistance from Malcolm MacDonald (p.103).

1948
Publishes *America and Cosmic Man*, a study of American history and society.

1949–51
Employed as Art Critic for *The Listener* and praises the work of Michael Ayrton, Francis Bacon and other young British painters.

1949
Works on a portrait of Eliot (p.105; p.107); is the subject of a retrospective exhibition at the Redfern Gallery, London.

1950
Publishes *Rude Assignment*, an autobiography.

1951
Announces his blindness in the final article he publishes as Art Critic for *The Listener*; publishes *Rotting Hill* (short stories based on life in England during the period of 'austerity' presided over by Sir Stafford Cripps (p.84).

1952
Publishes *The Writer and the Absolute* (essays on Jean Paul Sartre, André Malraux, Albert Camus and George Orwell).

1954
Publishes *Self Condemned*, a novel based on the Lewises' Canadian 'exile' in Toronto in 1940–3.

1955
A BBC broadcast dramatizes sequels to *The Childermass*, published as *The Human Age*, *Monstre Gai* and *Malign Fiesta*.

1956
Publishes *The Red Priest*, a novel about a boxing high churchman who kills his curate; is the subject of a retrospective exhibition at Tate (*Wyndham Lewis and Vorticism*).

1957
Lewis dies in Westminster Hospital, London on 7 March.

BURYING EUCLID DEEP IN THE LIVING FLESH

WYNDHAM LEWIS AND PORTRAITURE

CONTRADICT YOURSELF. IN ORDER TO LIVE, YOU MUST REMAIN BROKEN UP [1]

Towards the end of his life, blind and able to see his paintings only in his mind's eye, Wyndham Lewis wrote a short review of his career as a painter for the catalogue of the retrospective exhibition *Wyndham Lewis and Vorticism*. Vorticism was what Lewis was, and is still, most famous for – the avant-garde movement that he led in 1914, pioneering geometrical abstraction, composing manifestos and attempting to overturn the complacent traditionalism of British culture with the stunning magazine that he edited and designed, *Blast*. But in 1956 it was his work as a portraitist that Lewis singled out as a 'grand visual legacy', regretting only that he had not produced more: 'In my portraits what is lacking is numbers. I wish I had done fifty Macleods and Spenders.'[2]

This regret is perhaps misleading. Certainly he produced comparatively few oil portraits, but then there are comparatively few oil paintings in Lewis's work as a whole. Not only were many of his earlier paintings (including several important Vorticist canvases) destroyed or lost,[3] but the great majority of his works were executed on paper rather than canvas. Walter Michel's 1971 catalogue raisonné of Lewis's work records a total of only 127 oil paintings (including lost works), but well over 1000 works on paper. Many of these are portrait drawings, and as works of art are in no way inferior to the grander statements made by the large, definitive oil paintings that Lewis produced, often of the same subjects. Arguably, indeed, Lewis exploited his versatility with different media and his mastery of line to achieve a wider range of effects when working on paper than when he was confined to oil pigment and brush. In 1932 he wrote:

> It is always necessary to remember that oil paint, as used in the West (pigments mixed with oils, and applied to a strip of canvas or wood) does not possess any mystical advantage over images – representational or otherwise – done with lead or ink upon a strip of paper. Paper even has some notable advantages over canvas and wood, aside from the question of scale. Purer linear effects, especially of an improvisational nature, can be obtained with a dry pointed instrument upon a piece of paper, than with a wet and more blunt one upon a pigmented surface.[4]

We shall return to a discussion of Lewis's work on paper and oils on canvas. At present it is sufficient to say that the tradition he worked in demanded the scale and density of oil paintings for its public images of personalities, and, when called on to do so (or when he chose to do so) Lewis used the full resources of that tradition to an effect that he was justly proud of. The images he left us in this medium of Edith Sitwell (1887–1964), T.S. Eliot (1888–1965) and Ezra Pound (1885–1972) are definitive. Those of other associates, lovers and his wife, though history may not have demanded records of their appearance, have equal permanence as works of art. They are presentations of personalities we feel we can understand, and feel empathy for.

Praxitella
Wyndham Lewis
1920–1
Oil on canvas
1422 x 1016mm
(56 x 40in)
Leeds City
Galleries

Yet empathy is reputedly the 'wrong' objective for a modernist artist. According to artist and art critic Roger Fry (1866–1934), a man's head is no more and no less important than a pumpkin' when represented in a painting. And Lewis's own fictional surrogate, Tarr (the semi-autobiographical protagonist of his modernist novel, written between 1911 and 1915), explains that works of art have no 'inside', no 'restless ego' living in their interior, having instead a kind of 'dead' version of living through their forms and surfaces alone.[5]

Tarr simplifies his author's views, for in reality Lewis, while a modernist artist, scorned Fry's statement as simplistic and unrealistic. Even when closest to Fry's or Tarr's aesthetic desiderata, as in *Praxitella* (p.13) or *Portrait of the Artist as the Painter Raphael* (below and p.26), Lewis produced images to which we respond at least partly as if they were beings with an interior life. And despite Tarr's dogmatism and Lewis's own desire to throw over the tradition of naturalism, Lewis was capable of allowing quite contradictory objectives in his aesthetic, and his art flourished on such contradictions. Perhaps the contradiction, anyway, is in our understanding of modernism rather than in its own practice. This would account for our tendency to relegate portraiture to a corral of 'exceptions' outside the mainstream of modernist art history, even when practised by the greatest of painters. Lewis's own mature reflections on portraiture show how this may be a mistake, and how portraiture has an aesthetic, not just a sociological or an economic history:

The reality that is reflected in some portraits (but not I am afraid those painted very recently) is so fresh and delicate, as in the case of the great familiar portraits of the Renaissance, that it is, while you gaze at these reflections, like living yourself, in a peculiar immortality.... A portrait evidently ceases to be a portrait when it has that transporting effect that makes you feel, not only that you are sharing a moment of life removed by centuries from your own lifetime, but also that you are participating in a heightened life, the living of which only is an event as solitary and fixed as the thing at which you are gazing.[6]

For Lewis, such an experience may also be derived from 'abstract proportions and shape, merely, of a pictorial composition ... apart from its human reference', but this leads him not to dismiss 'human reference' from his aesthetic, but to state that 'there is a much closer relationship ... between the most "representative" and the most "abstract" painter, than is generally supposed'.[7] Lewis himself had no problem with practising abstraction and non-naturalistic invention alongside the apparent naturalism of his portraiture. The geometric abstraction was still there as the skeletal structure of the painting, but, in his famous phrase, by virtue of 'burying Euclid deep in the living flesh'.[8]

If a lingering aesthetic uneasiness about portraiture has marginalized it, there are yet other reasons why Lewis's own work in the genre may seem surprising – even baffling – to anyone who knows of him only

Portrait of the Artist as the Painter Raphael Wyndham Lewis 1921 Oil on canvas 763 x 686mm (30 x 27in.) Manchester City Galleries

William Shakespeare (detail) Martin Droeshout 1623 or 1663–4 Engraving 191 x 159mm (7½ x 6¼in.) National Portrait Gallery, London (NPG 185)

by reputation. As a writer he is 'known' mainly as an unsparing satirist, and as a racist, misogynistic homophobe who was also a fascist. Of all the generation of 'reactionary' modernists, Lewis has the worst reputation. How could such a man be responsible for the portrait drawing of Rebecca West (p.79) or the 1937 painting of Froanna (p.95)? Even if the charges against him were considerably softened (and a close study of his writing reveals them to be crass oversimplifications), the disparity remains.

Such a disparity was, at its most general, quite programmatic and intentional on Lewis's part. In the deepest sense he was a pluralist, aware that no single, completely coherent personality could reflect the full range of truth about anything, for truth is multiple, contradictory and always partial. The multiplicity of Lewis's own media of expression reflects this, giving rise to novels, satires, short stories, poems, literary and aesthetic theory and criticism, sociological investigation, autobiography, metaphysical speculation, political theory, cultural criticism, theological fantasy and polemical commentary on current affairs – over forty books in all, as well as countless essays and articles. Alongside this, and in some ways even more fundamental, were the kinds of truths available to the visual artist, reordering the raw data of visual experience and re-imagining it with heightened human significance.

Lewis was never content to be merely 'one thing' or reducible to a unity, and his idea of personal identity was therefore also something multiple and contradictory. Any self-presentation could be provisional, strategic or ironic – 'The Enemy', 'Mr Wyndham Lewis as a Tyro' ('Tyros' were grinning puppets invented by Lewis for satirical purposes) or as 'the Painter Raphael', for example. Equally, those personalities that fascinated him or that he admired demanded a range of responses and different forms of truth-telling from him as an artist. The drawings in ink, chalk, wash or pencil of some of these sitters give us these alternative partial truths about them, truths that are inseparable from the particular manner in which the drawings were executed – energetically and incisively in tense linear arcs, with delicate pencil shading or grainy chalk, with confidently floated washes or with a calligraphic flourish. Aside from a few incidental touches, Lewis was not a satirist when it came to portraiture. He was capable of writing extremely wounding descriptions or criticisms of the same people whom, in portraits, he represented entirely sympathetically. Perhaps this is why he always insisted that his most fundamental relationship with the world was through the eye; his own seems to have been kinder than his heart, or than his linguistic imagination at least.

If Lewis's works on paper give us a range of visual truths, his major oil paintings aim to be more comprehensive. They produce their meanings by virtue of belonging to and modifying a 'tradition', just as T.S. Eliot prescribed for the major statements of modernist literature. Lewis's was a western tradition of portraiture, but much more as well, for he saw modern art as the unending invention of a complex language requiring a vocabulary, grammar and rhetoric appropriate for a rapidly changing and globalized world. No single tradition, any more than any unitary 'self', could encompass the truths of this world. He therefore drew upon every conceivable visual source to nourish his complex artistic imagination – from the Old Masters of the European tradition, medieval illuminated manuscripts and the great British caricaturists, to Pre-Columbian, African, Egyptian and Chinese art. From his own time he looked at, and learned from, everything from major modernist artists such as Pablo Picasso (1881–1973) and Umberto Boccioni (1882–1916) to Dadaist typography and cheap commercial art. Lewis's remarkable achievement was to create a unique style of his own which leaves complex traces of these encounters without ever losing the powerful imprint of his own creative personality. This visual promiscuity was part of the wider heroic, cultural and political concept he promoted for the role of the 20th-century artist, which included his work as a writer. Lewis saw himself as a priestly exponent of a 'primitive form of world art', a pioneer who was aware that 'the Earth has become one place, instead of a romantic tribal patchwork of places'.[9]

The consequences of this ambitious artistic and intellectual synthesis for Lewis's portraiture were fascinating and ever-changing, often evident in small details such as sitters' eyes and hands. From the harsh, often luridly glaring extremes of the 'Tyro' images of the 1920s, to the gentler tonalities with which he approached his sitters in the late 1930s, we find a restless and yet highly purposeful effort to renew the European tradition. In the alarmingly yellow- and feline-eyed

Praxitella, for instance, we see a primitive mask metallically transformed by an eerie electric-blue urban light. The figure itself, with its mechanically articulated fingers, has an Egyptian and hieratic fixity, yet the title invokes the Greek classical tradition. The strangely flat-eyed *Portrait of the Artist as the Painter Raphael*, with its title that draws a distinction between 'artist' and 'painter', refers to the classical revival of which Lewis was so suspicious in the early 1920s. Yet it seems to be drawn also from the famous Martin Droeshout (1601–50?) engraving of William Shakespeare for the 1623 First Folio (p.14), giving it an entirely different register of meaning. *Edith Sitwell* (p.43), her head suggestive of an iconic Elizabethan portrait, sits in a setting with classic Renaissance props such as books and a globe, her gaze apparently turned inward. By contrast the cubist shapes of the body, and the abstract arrangement of coloured patterns where the famous slender hands should be, hint at another world and time zone.

Lewis's celebrated portraits from 1937 to 1939 are no less complex in their visual language, though most do seem less radical at first sight. *Froanna (Portrait of the Artist's Wife)* (p.95) has a Hogarthian straightforwardness in the modelling of the head and the highlights of the eyes, but reinvented through an encounter with Matissian-drenched colour and the still lifes of the later 'metaphysical' art of Giorgio de Chirico (1888–1978) and Carlo Carrà (1881–1966). It also harks back, in the hands, to the traditional devices of Sir Anthony Van Dyck (1599–1641) and Sir Joshua Reynolds (1723–92). The *fin-de-siècle* bohemian *Ezra Pound* (p.63) floats in a dream world conjured up by J.M.W. Turner (1775–1851) and James Abbott McNeill Whistler (1834–1903), while strong hints of Chinese watercolour remind us of these two artists' passion for Oriental art and aesthetics. Below the massive sculpted head, Pound's arms flow into hands that in turn seem to merge with his legs, as though his mind and body were as fluid as the painted sea behind him.

With Lewis's magisterial head-on portrait of T.S. Eliot (p.69) we are faced with his apparently most traditionally 'European' work – and appropriately so, given the public aspirations signalled by its submission to the Royal Academy of Arts in 1938. The pale green, almost cinematic, screen onto which the poet's powerfully modelled head casts an enigmatic shadow evokes de Chirico's portrait of Apollinaire from 1914. As if to suggest entirely different ideas, however, on either side of the screen are extraordinary combinations of shapes in which glimpses of birds or angels and other heavenly forms remind us of the theological imagination lurking behind Eliot's dark, sharply drawn features. It might seem bizarre that this portrait should have been rejected by the Royal Academy, yet the Academicians had seen immediately and instinctively why it challenged what Lewis characterized as the simple flatteries of their 'chocolate-box' naturalism.

As the works in this book demonstrate, Lewis's portraits are always resolutely non-naturalistic and complex meditations on style and personality in a baffling world. They also have for us now an additional value: we go to them simply as portraits, works that have their own presence, evoking the reality of their sitters in a way that is quite different from what is achieved in photography. Lewis complained that portraiture in England had become a bastard offspring of the camera, and in his work he tried to restore, renew and transform the more traditional canons of visual art. Through Lewis's work we have a special, heightened and irreplaceable record of the personalities of some of the greatest creators of the first half of the 20th century, as well as of public figures from outside the arts. It is a matchless achievement in British art of its time.

Paul Edwards and Richard Humphreys

NOTES

1 Lewis, 1917, p.7.
2 Lewis, 1956, p.4. See p.85 for Lewis's portrait of Stephen Spender. The John McLeod portrait (1939, Michel M P83) is in the Yale Center for British Art.
3 Several of Lewis's paintings from the 1920s, such as the portrait of Edith Sitwell and *Praxitella*, seem to have been painted over Vorticist canvases.
4 Lewis, 1932, p.5.
5 For Fry: Roger Fry, 'The Artist's Vision', quoted in Lewis, 1919, p.333. For Tarr: Lewis, 1918, pp.299–300.
6 Lewis, 1922a, pp.68–9. The context indicates that the phrase 'a portrait ceases to be a portrait' means something like, 'a likeness ceases to be a mere likeness'.
7 Lewis, 1922a, p.70.
8 Lewis, 1939a, p.330.
9 Lewis, 1929b, p.259.

'MR WYNDHAM LEWIS'
PORTRAITS OF THE ARTIST

THE FLOURISHING AND BOMBASTIC ROLE THAT YOU MAY SOMETIMES SEE ME IN, THAT IS AN EFFECT OF CHANCE

OR IT IS A CARICATURE OF SOME CONSTANT FIGURE IN THE AUDIENCE, RATHER THAN WHAT I AM (IN ANY SENSE) MYSELF. OR, TO MAKE MYSELF CLEARER, IT IS MY OPPOSITE [1]

Image was always important to Wyndham Lewis, however ironically he adopted some of his roles. 'The Enemy' or the author of *Tarr*, or the 'Luther of Ossington Street' or even 'Captain Brown' (to a critic who inopportunely accosted him in a pub) – such roles and namings originated, it seems, as a strategy to circumvent youthful gaucheness. When Lewis first went to Paris at the age of twenty-two he quickly changed his appearance from a tweed-jacketed public schoolboy look to something more exotic and Latin. He was duly pleased to remain unrecognized by an old Slade School acquaintance even after ten minutes' chat in the street.

For Lewis, an image of himself, in art as well as life, tended to be an appearance to present to the world, a calculated statement, not a revelation of the hidden self. His numerous self-portraits are, as much as the clothes he chose or designed for himself – notably the trademark broad-brimmed black hat – constructed images.

Lewis's own personality was divided between opposing forces. But he believed in the need for a strong personality that could hold its own against fashions and ideologies. 'I have allowed these contradictory things to struggle together, and the group that has proved the most powerful I have fixed on as my most essential ME'[2] – but the 'ME' that emerged was never definitive.

It is striking, for example, that two widely divergent images of himself, *Mr Wyndham Lewis as a Tyro* (p.25) and *Portrait of the Artist as the Painter Raphael* (p.26) were both painted in the same year and both exhibited together in the 1921 *Tyros and Portraits* exhibition. But as well as presenting different versions of the self, they served different purposes in situating Lewis in relation to aspects of contemporary culture. Thus, at the same time as producing his self-portrait 'as a Tyro', Lewis issued a new avant-garde magazine, also called *The Tyro*. He described the invented figures in this magazine as 'laughing elementals' and 'immense novices', and depicted them breakfasting, being schooled and reading Ovid. In a project both literary and visual, Lewis intended to provide a satirical anatomy of society after the First World War, showing both the social after-effects of that huge shock and the kind of infantilized society (organized along syndicalist lines) that it might lead to – and Lewis himself is inescapably part of that new society.

By contrast, the placid *Portrait of the Artist as the Painter Raphael* responds to the 'call to order' and return to classicism in France after the First World War. Lewis disliked its reactionary conservatism, which ignored those aspects of culture he wished to anatomize in his populist 'Tyro' images. He mocked one of its chief propagandists, André Lhote: '"Raphael shall be avenged!" shrieks M. Lhote. I have heard ... that he is really very excited, and that the Madonna-like face of the Florentine master inspires him to a very great fury ... of idolatrous love.'[3] Lewis's self-image here has a classical calm, but is also an implicit rejection of the idea that a return to Raphael would be an adequate route to truths about the modern world.

Paul Edwards

NOTES

1 Lewis, 1930, p.125.
2 Lewis, 1927a, p.132.
3 Lewis, 1919, p.137.

SELF-PORTRAIT
1911

Pencil and watercolour
on paper
305 x 235mm
(12 x 9¼in.)
C.J. Fox

This is one of three cubist self-portraits produced in 1911, only one of which was exhibited during Lewis's lifetime. Having studied in Paris for four years, from 1904 until 1908, he still visited Paris regularly after he moved to London, and he watched artistic developments there closely. It was the potential of cubism for radical simplification and stark monumentality that evidently appealed to him. Lewis uses a cubist idiom in this portrait to emphasize his impersonal, slightly threatening gaze. Yet despite its architectonic quality, this head also dissolves into the indeterminate space that it inhabits.

W. Lewis.

SELF-PORTRAIT 1920

Pen and wash on paper
180 x 220mm
(7 x 8¾in.)
Private Collection

At the 1920 Group X exhibition, Lewis exhibited at least four self-portraits, one of which was an oil painting (now lost). Several of these self-portraits were produced using black ink, and could be mistaken for wood engravings. In this work from 1920, Lewis exploits a similar effect of strong chiaroscuro, supplemented by washes whose handling makes it impossible to mistake this particular drawing for a print. The face is constructed from almost, but not quite, symmetrical antitheses of dark and light shapes and marks, also echoed in the contrast in the lighting of left and right shoulders. For Lewis, a productive human identity was similarly dualistic. It was out of this argument between different sides of his personality that he created his art and writing.

MR WYNDHAM LEWIS AS A TYRO 1920–1

Oil on canvas
730 x 440mm
(28¾ x 17⅜in.)
Ferens Art Gallery,
Hull City Museums
and Art Gallery

Lewis's best-known self-portrait is a striking example of his use of portraiture to project a chosen identity rather than to reveal a 'self'. The title shows it to be at two removes from such a self – 'Mr Wyndham Lewis' refers to the public figure known as an avant-garde painter and novelist, while this figure is presented 'as a Tyro'. The grin of the Tyro can be seen as a kind of hysterical continuation into peacetime of the 'keep smiling' attitude instilled in the British Tommy in the First World War. With the war apparently forgotten, 'Mr Wyndham Lewis' faces the future with this brave British grin, but the sour and sickly colouring of the image hints that the terrible past is not so easily repressed.

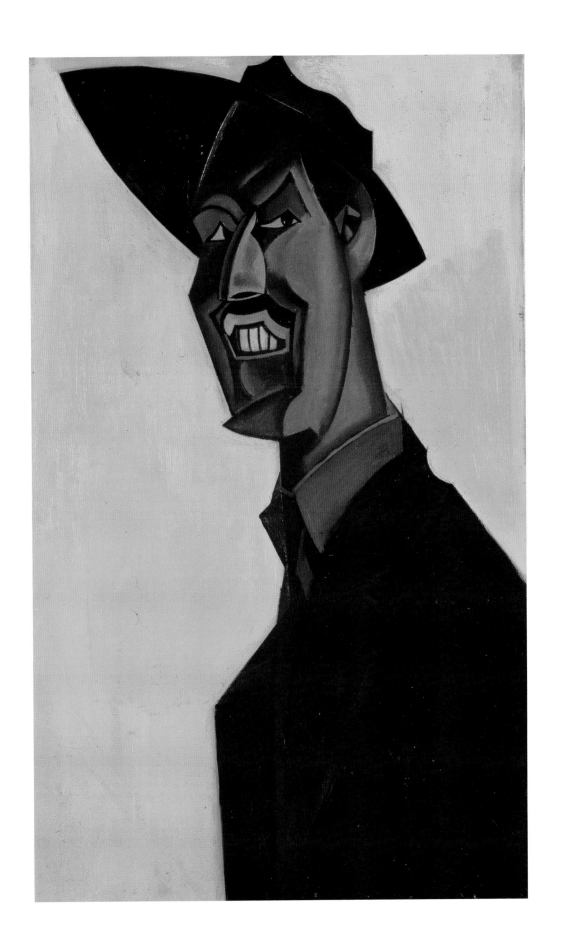

PORTRAIT OF THE ARTIST AS THE PAINTER RAPHAEL
1921

Oil on canvas
763 x 686mm
(30 x 27in.)
Manchester City
Galleries

Almost as starkly simplified as *Mr Wyndham Lewis as a Tyro* (p.25), this version of Lewis's self carries quite different connotations, though it too was shown in the 1921 *Tyros and Portraits* exhibition. This self-portrait might just be interpreted as a mirror-image version of Raphael's head and shoulders in *The School of Athens* (1511), but a more immediate model is the familiar engraved portrait of Shakespeare by Martin Droeshout (p.14), used as a frontispiece for the First Folio collection of his works in 1623. There is a 'classical' serenity in the image, but the painting is laying claim to an English classicism, rather than the French version of a classical tradition that Lewis found inappropriate to the modern world. Lewis elsewhere commented on Shakespeare's 'serene and empty' countenance, which concealed a profound internal drama.

SELF-PORTRAIT WITH HAT 1930

Pencil and wash
on paper
290 x 203mm
(11½ x 8in.)
Private Collection

By 1930 Lewis was better known as a writer than a painter, having published nine books and three issues of his predominantly literary magazine, *The Enemy*, since 1925. His broad-brimmed sombrero was an essential part of his role as 'Enemy' of the spuriously revolutionary in contemporary culture. As part of a sales drive for the limited edition of his 1930 satire, *The Apes of God*, Lewis produced a broadside: 'BUY THE APES OF GOD AND SEE FOR YOURSELF WHAT THIS IS ALL ABOUT!'. The single leaf included a reproduction of this self-portrait. Characteristically, Lewis chose to use a drawing that hints at a vulnerability that is at odds with the unsparing aggression of the satire directed by his novel at the art world.

SELF-PORTRAIT WITH HAT
1932

Pen, ink and wash
on paper
254 x 197mm
(10 x 7¾in.)
National Portrait Gallery,
London (NPG 4528)

This is another image associated
with Lewis's 'Enemy' role.
A reproduction of this drawing
accompanied an article written by
Lewis as a piece of self-advertisement
in the *Daily Herald*: 'What it feels
like to be an Enemy' (30 May 1932).
The drawing is an object lesson in
the way illusion may be created by
flat washes and strokes of the pen.
In this sense the artist's apparent
enjoyment of his own resourceful
artifice may also comment on the
element of make-believe in Lewis's
self-dramatization as 'The Enemy'.

SELF-PORTRAIT 1932

Pencil on paper,
330 x 255mm
(13 x 10in.)
Private Collection

One of a series of highly finished pencil heads that Lewis produced for his 1932 exhibition, *Thirty Personalities*, this self-portrait was reproduced in his portfolio published the same year, *Thirty Personalities and a Self Portrait*. Lewis believed that the draughtsmanship was not as 'traditional' as it seemed at first sight. Given the differences between pen-and-ink and pencil, the drawing is as 'constructed' and synthetic as the highly calligraphic *Self-portrait with Hat* (p.27). Lewis insisted that visual art used a 'language', and this drawing is made from visual 'signs' that keep it from becoming simply naturalistic. The personality presented here is not Lewis the bohemian artist or 'Enemy', but a sober, lounge-suited figure.

SELF-PORTRAIT WITH PIPE

1938

Pencil on paper
495 x 385mm
(19½ x 15¼in.)
The Poetry Collection of
the University Libraries,
State University of
New York at Buffalo

Self-portrait with Pipe is Lewis's last recorded self-portrait, featuring the Peterson pipe that is also prominent in photographs taken in April 1938 during the controversy over the Royal Academy's rejection of his portrait of T.S. Eliot (p.69). The self-portrait was probably intended to accompany an article, 'Fifty Years of Painting', on Sir William Rothenstein's retrospective exhibition of that title, which was held six months after the rejection controversy. The article, instead of being satirical and extending Lewis's feud with the Royal Academy, was sober and appreciative of Rothenstein's paintings, and perhaps for this reason was not published – although it did eventually appear in *Apollo* (Lewis, 1938c). War was approaching and with it new roles that did not require visual self-dramatization. Lewis was the 'Enemy' no longer.

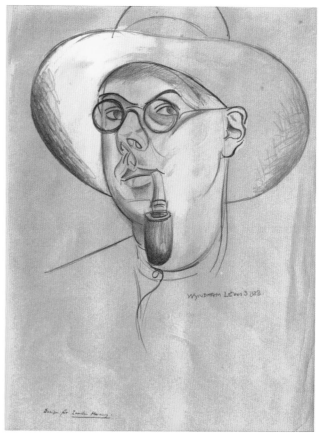

APES AND FAMILIARS

THE ART WORLD OF THE 1920s

IT IS TO WHAT I HAVE CALLED THE APES OF GOD THAT I AM DRAWING YOUR ATTENTION

THOSE PROSPEROUS
MOUNTEBANKS
WHO ALTERNATELY
IMITATE AND MOCK
AT AND TRADUCE
THOSE FIGURES THEY
AT ONCE ADMIRE
AND HATE [1]

In the 1920s, Lewis found it impossible to achieve for his art the kind of notoriety and publicity that Vorticism had commanded before the First World War. His *Tyros and Portraits* exhibition made little impact, his money ran out, and he failed to complete the necessary complement of advanced experimental works needed for a projected show in Léonce Rosenberg's gallery L'Effort Moderne in Paris. In England, the Bloomsbury Group, with whom he had quarrelled before the war, imposed its critical values on the art world, to Lewis's cost. At the same time, as an avant-garde writer he was being eclipsed by James Joyce and T.S. Eliot. Lewis was thrown back on the patronage of friends who were also practising writers and artists, sometimes raising money through portrait commissions from them. But, always suspicious of the motives of those who were prepared to help him, Lewis found the patronage of people he considered his artistic inferiors intolerable. Portraits were sometimes left unfinished.

Sidney Schiff, a generous patron who was also a novelist, commissioned a portrait of his wife (*Mrs Schiff*, p.51), but found dealing with Lewis exasperating. He finally extricated it, still not quite completed, from the artist in 1926. Schiff told Lewis that he would never again enter a business relationship with any artist, 'least of all with you', adding that this was because his 'lasting admiration and underlying regard' for him were 'unchangeable and must never be exposed to assault'.[2]

Lewis gradually withdrew from the art world and reduced the amount of painting he was doing. He undertook a massive reading programme on political theory, anthropology and philosophy, and re-launched his career in 1926 as a writer in a series of books of cultural criticism underpinned by this reading. In a new magazine he also developed a new persona, 'the Enemy'. The culmination of these campaigns, and his fullest revenge on his associates of the 1920s, was a massive satire on artistic London, *The Apes of God*, published in 1930. Prominent among those satirized were several of the sitters in the present section of the exhibition. Despite Lewis's devastating satire of the Schiffs, they remained generous to him, regretting the loss of his friendship. The longest chapter in the book, 'Lord Osmund's Lenten Party', is an extended satire of the Sitwell family. In his 1937 autobiography, *Blasting and Bombardiering*, Lewis hinted at the paradoxical fellowship that underlay his public enmity with Edith Sitwell: 'We are two good old enemies, Edith and I, inseparables in fact. I do not think I should be exaggerating if I described myself as Miss Edith Sitwell's *favourite enemy*.'[3]

Lewis explained that his first successful writing came about when he was making a portrait of a blind beggar: 'the "short story" was the crystallization of *what I had to keep out of my consciousness while painting*.'[4] He felt that other painter–writers – notably William Blake (1757–1827) and Dante Gabriel Rossetti (1828–82) – had not managed their dual talents well, 'because their two selves were upon too intimate terms with one another'.

Remarkably, the resentments towards his friends and patrons that were building up during the 1920s were successfully kept out of the portraits themselves. And in Lewis's writing, although these resentments may be the foundation for the satire, what Lewis builds upon them is of far more significance than mere personal grudges. *The Apes of God* is a diagnosis of the cultural failure of modernism in the period after the First World War, a depiction of the process by which experiment in the arts declined into mere lifestyle. The narrative culminates in a representation of the 1926 General Strike, and a paralysed London rather than one electrified by the revolutionary fervour of avant-garde art.

Paul Edwards

NOTES

1 Lewis, 1930, p.125.
2 Quoted in O'Keeffe, 2000, p.267.
3 Lewis, 1937a, p.96.
4 Lewis, 1935, p.266.

L'INGÉNUE
1919

Pencil, red chalk
and wash
510 x 350mm
(20 x 13¾in.)
Manchester City
Galleries

Iris Barry (1895–1969, born Frieda Crump) came to London in search of a literary career after a correspondence with Lewis's friend, Ezra Pound. Lewis lived with Iris from 1918 to 1921, during which time she gave birth to two children, Robin and Maisie. Iris is reported to have said that Lewis was the only man never to have bored her. She later became the curator of the Film Archive of the Museum of Modern Art in New York.

Lewis in 1919 was dissatisfied with the draughtsmanship of his war work and devoted himself to figure drawing in order to perfect his 'hand'. The linear mastery he achieved became the foundation for the inventive abstractions he now produced, as well as for the figuration and portrait works of the early 1920s. Lewis manages to achieve not only impressive formal effects, but also a sense of a human personality – signalled in this case by the unusual title.

WOMAN KNITTING 1920

Pencil on paper
502 x 325mm
(19¾ x 12¾in.)
Manchester City
Galleries

Iris passed the time knitting while pregnant with Maisie, and even thought of starting a business knitting clothes. Lewis wanted his figurative work to show some of the qualities of formal abstraction and this drawing, with its precise arcs and angles, is reminiscent of the shapes found in his pre-First World War Vorticist abstractions. It was quite customary for Lewis at this time to leave areas of his drawings – in this case the chair – in a loose, apparently unfinished state, in contrast with other areas that were worked to a high degree of finish.

STUDY FOR PAINTING (SEATED LADY)
1920

Pencil, wash
and gouache
375 x 275mm
(14¾ x 10¾in.)
Manchester City
Galleries

This study of Iris Barry was reproduced in Lewis's 1950 autobiography *Rude Assignment*, entitled *Cave Woman in a Chair*. It is a preparatory study for the major oil portrait *Praxitella* (p.13), which was exhibited in Lewis's 1921 *Tyros and Portraits* exhibition. The painting, with its odd title, may, like the *Portrait of the Artist as the Painter Raphael* (p.26), be a response to the revival of classicism in France after the First World War. In the study, Iris wears the same dress as in the painting (with the addition of a wrap-over waistcoat often worn with it), but has a more 'African' variant of stylized mask for her head. The viewpoint is much higher than in the painting, and the alternative title reveals that Lewis saw this work as expressing a more primitive dynamism than the finished painting, which, for all its stylistic extremism, retains a 'classical' immobility and otherworldliness.

MARY WEBB (GIRL LOOKING DOWN) 1919

Black chalk on paper
290 x 370mm
(11½ x 14½in.)
Private Collection

Mary Webb (1881–1927) was the author of several romantic novels set in Shropshire, such as *Gone to Earth* (1917) and *Precious Bane* (1924). Her love of rural life and feeling for the mysterious power of nature would seem to be remote from Lewis's sympathies, but the portrait is a kind one. Webb suffered from Graves' disease (a disorder of the thyroid), causing a goitre and bulging eyes. This may explain the pose Lewis has chosen for this drawing. As with the contemporaneous *L'Ingénue* (p.35), some areas – particularly the head, bow-tie and buttons – are worked to a higher degree of finish than others. The sitter's slightly unruly hair indicates a character belied by the neatness of her dress.

EDWARD WADSWORTH 1920

Black chalk and wash
on paper
305 x 280mm
(12 x 11in.)
Junior Common Room
Art Collection of
Pembroke College,
Oxford

Edward Wadsworth (1889–1949) was a fellow Vorticist, the painter that Lewis thought best understood the spirit of the movement's engagement with the machine age. After the First World War Wadsworth inherited a fortune derived from his family's factories in the north of England, and he was one of the group of friends who supported Lewis with a monthly allowance during a period of poverty in the early 1920s. Along with the others, he duly found himself and his wife satirized in *The Apes of God*, where he appears as a 'horsy motorist, in giant scotch-checks' who utters exclamations 'with emphatic traces of trenchant Yorkshire, with a false nail-driving heartiness'. Lewis rejected his first attempt at this drawing and inverted the sheet. The construction of Wadsworth's foreshortened right arm and leg is typical of Lewis's rhythmical use of free-hand arcs and scallop shapes at this period.

EDITH SITWELL

1921

Pencil and
watercolour
on paper
395 x 260mm
(15½ x 10¼in.)
Trustees of the
Cecil Higgins Art
Gallery, Bedford

Edith Sitwell (1887–1964) is now best
remembered as the author of the poems set
to music in *Façade*, by Sir William Walton,
in 1922. Lewis was closely associated with
Edith and her brothers during the early
1920s, but seems not to have regarded
her poetry with any respect. In *The Apes
of God*, one of the characters dismisses
a book by a society poetess modelled on
Edith: 'All about arab rocking-horses of the
true Banbury Cross breed. Still making
mud-pies at forty!' (Lewis, 1930, p.494).
But Lewis's portraits pay her the tribute
of expressing quite varying aspects of
her personality. She believed herself to
be ugly, distracting attention from this
by her choice of dress, jewellery and
headdress. Only her hands, she thought,
had any natural elegance. Here Lewis has
eliminated all her defensive accoutrements
and recorded unsparingly her visual
appearance, but the result is sympathetic.
He has even included a hand.

EDITH SITWELL
1921

Pencil on paper
387 x 286mm
(15¼ x 11¼in.)
National Portrait Gallery,
London (NPG 4464)

Edith Sitwell claimed that she sat for Lewis every day except Sundays for ten months for the oil portrait he painted of her (opposite). Sittings began in late 1921. The work illustrated here is evidently a preparatory drawing in which Lewis concentrated on the formalization of the structure of the head, a feature of all his oil portraits from this period. In a letter to artist Sir William Rothenstein (quoted in Lewis, 1963), Lewis explained his method: 'I go primarily for the pattern of the structure of the head and insinuate, rather than stress, the "psyche".' In this case, the psychological damage of Edith Sitwell's cruel upbringing, and the tragic aspect of her self-display, are hinted at by the contrasting shapes of the eyes. Femininity is present only in the sensitively drawn mouth.

EDITH SITWELL 1923–35

Oil on canvas
864 x 1118mm
(34 x 44in.)
Tate. Presented
by Sir Edwards
Beddington-Behrens
1943

The painting was still unfinished in October 1923, when the debt-burdened Lewis did a moonlight flit from his studio in Kensington's Adam and Eve Mews. The head was complete, and the chair, coat and legs were more or less finished – the background was completed in 1935. The portrait thus spans Lewis's friendship and subsequent enmity with Edith. In other portraits up to this time his backgrounds were plain, in order to concentrate attention on the head. Here the head is silhouetted against the darkest panel in the painting. There is a great deal of visual activity in the lower half of the painting, but the beautifully modelled head has no visual competition in the upper part, and the viewer's gaze continually returns to it. This, along with the eyes almost closed, increases the sense that the sitter is isolated from the room that apparently defines her by its symbols of culture.

EDITH SITWELL
1923

Pencil and wash
on paper
400 x 289mm
(15¾ x 11⅜in.)
National Portrait Gallery,
London (NPG 4465)

In *The Apes of God*, at Lord Osmund's
party, a character declares of Harriet
Finnian Shaw (Edith Sitwell): 'There is
a celebrated painting of Battista Sforza
Duchess of Urbino. Harriet thinks she
looks like the portrait. Tonight she is got
up to look like the portrait.' In the present
work there are indeed subtle echoes of
Piero della Francesca's famous profile
portrait of the Duchess (1465–66). There
is not merely a facial resemblance (in the
eyes, for instance); the bunching of the hair
at the side of the head and the decorative
headband are also similar, without being
identical. Edith wears the same crucifix as
in Lewis's earlier portrait of her (p.43).

VIRGINIA WOOLF
1921

Pencil and wash
on paper
380 x 255mm
(15 x 10in.)
Victoria & Albert
Museum

There is no record in Woolf's journals of her having sat for Lewis, so the identity of the sitter in this portrait remains in question. The Bloomsbury Group epitomized the characteristics of Lewis's 'Apes of God', being, in his view, wealthy amateurs usurping the place of better painters and writers. Lewis had quarrelled with Woolf's friend Roger Fry in 1913 over a commission that Fry had secured at Lewis's expense. Twenty years later, in *Men Without Art* (1934), Lewis mocked Woolf's *Mrs Dalloway* (1925) for lacking the 'realistic vigour' of Joyce's *Ulysses* (1922), 'though often the incidents … are exact and puerile copies of the scenes in his Dublin drama' (Lewis, 1934, p.168). And in his novel, *The Revenge for Love* (1937), he attacked the 'highbrow feminist fairyland' of *A Room of One's Own* (1929) for its distracting irrelevance to a woman in real economic distress. Yet in his drawing, Lewis treated the sitter sympathetically.

EDWIN EVANS

1922

Oil on canvas
1500 x 1080mm
(59 x 42½in.)
National Galleries
of Scotland

Edwin Evans (1874–1945) was an
important music critic, some of whose
friends and admirers commissioned this
portrait in his honour. They were unable
to raise the full sum agreed from
subscribers to the project and Lewis
tailored his work to the flow of incoming
money, finally handing the portrait over
in its unfinished state. Although Lewis
professed comparative ignorance of music,
he had numerous acquaintances in the
field, producing portraits of Arthur Bliss
and Constant Lambert, and designing the
cover for the published score of Bliss's
Colour Symphony (1924).

MRS WORKMAN
1923

Pencil and wash
on paper
330 x 470mm
(13 x 18½in.)
Private Collection

Lewis recorded in his 1937 autobiography, *Blasting and Bombardiering*, how he would visit the house of the 'magnate, Workman ... with its windows in Park Lane' in the early 1920s. *Who's Who* records only one unlikely Canadian magnate by the name of Workman – Mark Workman (1881–1980), domiciled in Montreal. Lewis contrasts Workman's taste for slumberous pictures of Highland cattle with Mrs Workman's rare understanding of French painting 'of which she had some remarkably fine specimens' (Lewis, 1937a, pp.230–1). Like the drawing of Nancy Cunard opposite and several others that Lewis produced of society women in 1923, this work relies on delicacy of shading and wash rather than bold linearity. The geometrical structure that was so important to Lewis is present in the overall composition, with the figure on the chaise longue forming a pyramid in the centre of the sheet. Mrs Workman's taste for French art may have stimulated Lewis to emulate the portrait drawings of Jean Auguste Dominique Ingres (1780–1867).

NANCY CUNARD
1922

Pencil, watercolour
and pastel on paper
514 x 330mm
(20¼ x 13in.)
British Council

The boyish figure in cloche hat is the archetypal image of the emancipated woman of the 1920s. Nancy Cunard (1896–1965) was the daughter of shipping magnate Sir Bach Cunard. A poet and writer, she became a committed champion of the civil rights movement, editing an important anthology, *Negro* (1934). Lewis may have come to know Nancy through their shared association with the Sitwells. They had a love affair in 1922, and Lewis caricatured her affectionately as Baby Bucktrout in his satire on literary prizes and reviewing, *The Roaring Queen*, in 1931 (Lewis, 1973). Although it is difficult to generalize about a developing style in Lewis's art, the period 1919 to 1923 shows him moving from a bold and energetic linearity in his drawing (sometimes filled with limited areas of wash or shading to describe volume) to a more refined style, in which outline is likely to be defined by the boundaries of more subtly shaded or tinted areas.

MRS SCHIFF

1923–4

Oil on canvas
1257 x 1003mm
(49½ x 39½in.)
Tate.
Purchased 1956

Violet Zillah Beddington (1874–1962) married Sidney Schiff in 1914. She encouraged him in his literary ambitions, and both were generous patrons of artists and writers. Occupying the centre of the canvas, the head's warm colours contrast with the surrounding cool blues. An impression of upward movement and forward projection is created by the converging light blue lines of the dress and by the figure's position – cut off by the bottom and left-hand canvas edges, with a hand 'outside' the frame. The blue background, seeming also to extend beyond the canvas, balances the shape of the figure. However, the clarity and sculptural definition that made Lewis's other work of the 1920s so impressive remains unachieved in this unfinished work, except in the head. Lewis's satirical description of Isabel Kein (based on Violet Schiff) in *The Apes of God*, seated in an armchair, is clearly based on observations made during sittings for this portrait (Lewis, 1930, p.250).

SACHEVERELL SITWELL 1922

Pencil on paper
370 x 280mm
(14½ x 11in.)
Private Collection

Youngest brother of Edith, Sacheverell Sitwell (1897–1988) was a poet and author. In 1921 Lewis provided the cover illustration for Sitwell's poem, 'Dr Donne and Gargantua'. Lewis regarded Sacheverell as 'quite the nicest' of the Sitwells, and of 'literary lions' in general, but did not spare him from satirical caricature in *The Apes of God*, singling out his 'Fauntleroy' manner, his doe-like movements and his 'baldish and widow's-peaked' hair: 'A hyacinthine lock danced giglotish upon his tall and pensive temples as he leapt past in fawn-like awkwardness'. Lewis was staying in Venice as a guest of Nancy Cunard (p.49) when he drew this sympathetic portrait.

MEN OF 1914

EZRA POUND
JAMES JOYCE
T.S. ELIOT

WE ARE THE FIRST MEN OF A FUTURE THAT HAS NOT MATERIALIZED[1]

When Wyndham Lewis satirized people like the Sitwells, Sidney Schiff and Virginia Woolf as wealthy amateurs and imitators, it was by the highest standards that he did so. Ezra Pound, T.S. Eliot, James Joyce and Lewis himself – the 'Men of 1914', as he called them in his 1937 autobiography, *Blasting and Bombardiering* – were the pre-eminent innovators in the transition to unalloyed modernism in English literature. Pound had been Lewis's closest literary ally during the period of Vorticism, and produced a literary aesthetic for the movement that was somewhat different to Lewis's. Eliot's first publication in England was in the second issue of *Blast*, the 'War Number' issued in 1915; Joyce had been 'blessed' in the first.

The impresario for this grouping was Pound. While Lewis was in the Royal Garrison Artillery during the First World War, Pound ensured that all four, as well as other writers he wished to promote, appeared regularly in the small-circulation New York magazine, *The Little Review*. But none of them (including Lewis himself) ever achieved the ideal of a truly emancipated and genuinely revolutionary literary effort that Lewis regarded as the goal of writing. They were – or should have been – writing for that 'Future' that

Lewis was to decide, in 1937 on the brink of another world war, would not be achieved.

In 1919 Lewis had explained his vision, talking particularly of the visual transformation that avant-garde art should make:

> Simply for human life at all, or what sets out to be human life – *to increase gusto and belief in that life* – it is of the first importance that the senses should be directed into such channels, appealed to in such ways, that this state of mind of relish, fullness and exultation should obtain.[2]

More generally, he wrote that 'life as interpreted by the poet or philosopher is the objective of Revolution, they are the substance of its Promised Land'.[3] In the 1920s, as these dreams seemed to recede, Lewis became more convinced that, even in the work of the 'Men of 1914', there was a lack of truly critical thought, so that their work became an unwitting carrier of ideologies that thwarted social transformation. He therefore criticized his old associates – typically with more gusto than necessary – on the basis that:

My conception of the role of the creative artist is not merely to be a medium for ideas supplied to him wholesale from elsewhere, which he incarnates automatically in a technique which (alone) it is his business to perfect. It is equally his business to know enough of the sources of his ideas, and ideology, to take steps to keep these ideas out, except such as he requires for his work.[4]

The 'ideology' that Lewis was especially concerned with here is what he called 'time philosophy', a modern metaphysics he found in such writers as A.N. Whitehead (1861–1947) and Henri Bergson (1859–1941), which he regarded as inherently fatalistic and disempowering, and which he identified in the work of his old associates.

By the late 1930s this critique was no longer relevant, and Lewis had slipped into commemorative mode. His autobiography, laced with sardonic comedy, memorialized his relations with these other writers, while his 1938–9 portraits of Eliot and Pound did the same, but in a more monumental and definitive way. There was no equivalent late portrait of Joyce, for whatever reason. Relations between Lewis and Joyce cooled after his criticisms of Joyce's writing, and were perhaps not warm enough for him to make an approach. Joyce's residence in Paris would also have made producing a full-scale oil portrait difficult.

In his drawings of these friends, Lewis tended to favour particular media to suit his feeling for their personalities. When portraying Pound, he would go for the firm black line of black crayon or rougher black chalk. With Eliot he chose a hard graphite pencil for a more nuanced and delicate result. Joyce, on the other hand, elicited pen and ink that required both precision and virtuosity.

When Lewis submitted his autobiography to his publisher, it was suggested to him that he had devoted too much space to Eliot, Joyce and Pound. He replied:

In all arts and sciences there are a few men, a very few, whose views on each other's work are of substantial and enduring importance ... which will not be allowed to vanish, which will be quoted and reprinted for the sake of a percipience that is rare. Conversely, there is a large number of others who play a humble though not necessarily dishonourable part in dissemination, and whose views are of only commercial importance. If you are not able to grasp this distinction ... you would be better employed in the grocery trade.[5]

With his portraits of these writers Lewis could take the same pride, and we may rejoice in our good fortune in still being able to see them through the artist's eyes. These are not only great works of art in their own right, but unique records of one of the most important moments in 20th-century literature. But when they were produced, official culture had no time for them. The 1938 portrait of Eliot (p.69) was submitted to the Royal Academy and promptly rejected, confirming Lewis's opinion that that institution was itself engaged in a trade not much more elevated than grocery. As he wrote in 1950, it was 'a group of small-time businessmen – portrait painting (or horse-painting), now the only lucrative line that remains, who trade under a Royal Charter, in rent-free premises in the centre of Piccadilly'.[6]

Lewis had always been contemptuous of the Royal Academy, and his motives in submitting his painting of T.S. Eliot are not clear. He said the submission was a 'test case'. Eliot was at the time Britain's most prominent man of letters, and also dominated literary opinion in America. He had cultivated an aura of respectability that neither Lewis nor Pound wished to acquire. Nevertheless, Lewis may have reasoned, if the condition of public culture were as it should be, a quasi-official portrait of Eliot by a painter of Lewis's stature would be welcomed and given a prominent position in a major national gallery. The test Lewis set was not a difficult one, but the nation failed it; the portrait could find no public or private purchaser in England and was sold to a provincial gallery in South Africa for £250.

Paul Edwards

NOTES

1 Lewis, 1937a, p.258.
2 Lewis, 1919, p.30.
3 Lewis, 1927a, p.24.
4 Lewis, 1927a, p.136.
5 Lewis, in a letter to Douglas Jerrold, quoted in O'Keeffe, 2000, p.372.
6 Lewis, 1950b, p.358.

EZRA POUND 1919

Charcoal on paper
370 x 324mm
(14½ x 12¾in.)
Harry Ransom Center.
The University of Texas
at Austin

American poet Ezra Pound, then resident
in London, managed Lewis's literary affairs
while he was serving in the First World
War. A tireless and generous promoter of
the work of other writers and painters,
Pound had been the main organizing force
behind the publication of Eliot, Joyce and
Lewis himself. In the process, his lack
of tact led to more and more avenues of
publication for himself being closed off.
In 1919 Lewis signalled the renewal of
their alliance by painting an over life-size
portrait of Pound as a modern *condottiere*
and exhibiting it in the Goupil Salon, where
it was judged by one critic to be 'large
and intimidating, like the great figures
of Andrea del Castagno'. Unhappy with
it himself, Lewis probably destroyed the
work. This drawing, which matches the
force of Pound's personality with its own
decisive vigour, is probably part of the
preparatory work for the portrait.

EZRA POUND 1920

Crayon on paper
361 x 270mm
(14¼ x 10⅝in.)
National Portrait Gallery,
London (NPG 6728)

Ezra Pound had become disenchanted
with London by 1920, despairing of it
as a home for the literary renaissance
he had worked for. He left for Paris,
leaving T.S. Eliot and Lewis to continue
campaigning in London. Lewis left the
eyes in this drawing blank, something
he often did in order to emphasize that
the life of a work of art is in a different
realm from that of nature. To animate
the gaze of the sitter would give the
portrait what he called 'the wrong
kind of life'. The life in this drawing
is emphatically in the gusto of the
whiplash lines.

EZRA POUND 1921

Black chalk
on paper
370 x 320mm
(14$\frac{1}{2}$ x 12$\frac{5}{8}$in.)
Private Collection

The drawing was probably executed in 1920 (even though the work is inscribed with the date 1921) before Ezra Pound left London (there is a related drawing, dated 1920, in Manchester City Galleries; Lewis occasionally post-dated his work). Like several other of Lewis's drawings of seated figures, this exploits the potential of foreshortening afforded by the artist's viewpoint. The drawing becomes an opportunity for the display of Lewis's virtuoso line. In the second issue of *Blast*, Lewis described Pound as a 'Demon pantechnicon driver, busy with removal of old world into new quarters' ('American Art' in Lewis, 1915, p.82). The energy of the line in this drawing is an implicit homage to Pound's dynamism, animated even when at rest in an armchair.

Wyndham Lewis. 1921.

Drawing of EZRA POUND.

EZRA POUND 1938

Black crayon
on paper
330 x 255mm
(13 x 10in.)
Private Collection

Pound visited London in 1938 following the death of his mother-in-law, Olivia Shakespear. Possibly as a companion-piece to his portrait of T.S. Eliot, Lewis undertook an uncommissioned portrait, for which this is a study of the head. Lewis and Pound had drifted apart artistically since the early 1920s, though Pound continued to offer Lewis support from his new base in Rapallo, Italy. Lewis, though he had himself been taken in by Hitler for a few years, was sceptical of Pound's enthusiasm for Mussolini. He thought that Pound was unable to understand the realities of the present, even though he possessed an intuitive understanding of the remote past.

Wyndham Lewis.
1938.

EZRA POUND 1939

Oil on canvas
762 x 1016mm
(30 x 40in.)
Tate.
Purchased 1939

In his 1950 memoir of Pound, Lewis pointed out Pound's affinity with James Abbott McNeill Whistler and Thomas Carlyle (1795–1881): 'That Pound was conscious of the affinity is suggested by the frontispiece to *Pavannes and Divisions*, in which he is posed in raking silhouette, his overcoat trailing in reminiscence of Carlyle (though with swagger and rhetoric)' (Lewis, 1950a, pp.262–3). This portrait echoes Whistler, though with a reckless bravura appropriate to Pound. The sea in the background is a late addition. It has a Chinese feel to it, but also may recall Carlyle's phrase for the revolutionary Robespierre ('seagreen Incorruptible'). Lewis called Pound 'a born revolutionary, a Trotsky of the written word' (Lewis, 1937a, p.285). In *Time and Western Man* he wrote that '[Pound] has really walked with Sophocles beside the Aegean; he has *seen* the Florence of Cavalcanti' (Lewis, 1927b, p.69); the painted sea may thus also represent the Aegean that Pound, with eyes closed, sees in his imagination. The Tate bought the portrait from Lewis in 1939, for the pitiful sum of £100.

JAMES JOYCE 1920

Pen and ink and
wash on paper
265 x 205mm
(10½ x 8in.)
Private Collection

Lewis met James Joyce for the first time in the summer of 1920, in the company of T.S. Eliot, who brought a parcel of clothes and old shoes from Pound as a result of Joyce's complaints of poverty. Lewis's account of the meeting and of Joyce's subsequent insistence on paying for meals and drinks is one of the funniest chapters in *Blasting and Bombardiering*. Joyce and Lewis got on well together and became drinking partners, but there was always rivalry between them, not least because Lewis's novel *Tarr* and Joyce's *A Portrait of the Artist as a Young Man* had been linked by both Pound and Eliot in reviews.

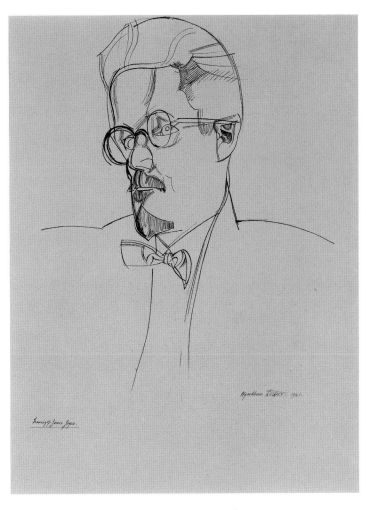

JAMES JOYCE 1921

Pen and ink
on paper
456 x 316mm
(17⅞ x 12½in.)
National Gallery
of Ireland, Dublin

This is Lewis's most naturalistic portrait of Joyce and one of his greatest drawings. Joyce's masterpiece of modernist literature, *Ulysses*, was virtually complete and Lewis must have known that he was portraying someone who (in his words) was 'a great literary artist'. He rose to the occasion. The work was owned by Joyce's admirer and patron, Harriet Shaw Weaver. It is a sign of Lewis's mastery of technique at this period of his life that he was able to reproduce the precision of his drawings in pencil and charcoal in the more exacting medium of pen and ink. A further drawing (reproduced in *Thirty Personalities and a Self Portrait*) is freer and more fluid in its delineation of Joyce's head, which Lewis described as 'a hollow hatchet'.

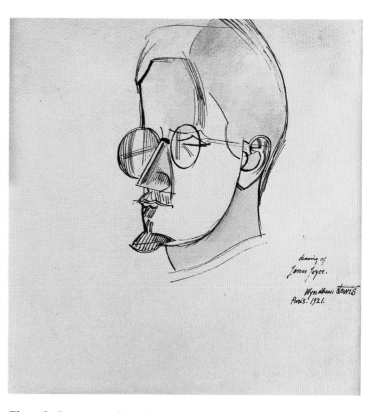

JAMES JOYCE 1921

Pen and ink and
wash on paper
282 x 206mm
(11¹⁄₈ x 8¹⁄₈in.)
Sheffield Galleries
and Museums Trust

Though Joyce may have learnt how to move beyond naturalism in his writing from Lewis's 1914 *Enemy of the Stars*, they were in truth very different as writers. Lewis criticized what he regarded as Joyce's conventionality of outlook (as opposed to technique): 'He is become so much a writing-specialist that it matters very little to him *what* he writes, or what idea or world-view he expresses, so long as he is trying his hand at this manner and that, and displaying his enjoyable virtuosity' (Lewis, 1927a, p.88). Joyce was offended, not least by several personal observations in Lewis's critique, and he incorporated his retaliation in his final novel, *Finnegans Wake* (1939), where Lewis is a major component in the Shaun archetype, while Joyce is the carefree scapegrace Shem.

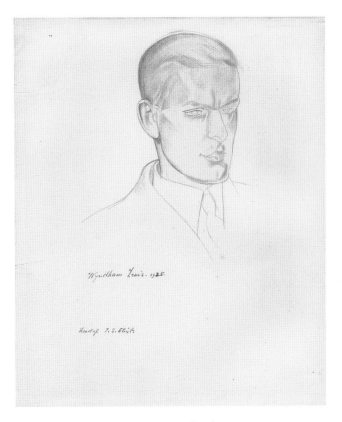

T.S. ELIOT
1925

Pencil and colour
on paper
310 x 256mm
(12¼ x 10in.)
Harry Ransom Center.
The University of Texas
at Austin

Lewis was introduced to T.S. Eliot by Ezra Pound not long after Eliot arrived in London from Germany after the outbreak of the First World War. In 1920 they holidayed in France together (where they first met Joyce). 'I do not know anyone more profitable to talk to', Eliot wrote to Sidney Schiff (Eliot, 1988, p.403). Eliot wrote for both issues of Lewis's magazine, *The Tyro*, and was anxious to publish Lewis in his own magazine, *The Criterion*. He helped Lewis by reading early drafts of what later became *Time and Western Man*, but Lewis took offence when Eliot did not print an essay in the issue of *The Criterion* he had announced it for. Eliot refused to allow this to spoil their friendship. In *Blasting and Bombardiering*, Lewis described Eliot's appearance when they first met in Pound's flat: 'A sleek, tall, attractive apparition – with a sort of Gioconda smile'.

T.S. ELIOT
1938

Oil on canvas
1333 x 851mm
(52½ x 33½in.)
Durban Municipal
Art Gallery

This is Lewis's most famous portrait – rejected by the Royal Academy in 1938. The Academy claimed to object to the elaborate 'scrolls' in the background, which of course had symbolic significance. The left-hand scroll contains a phallic form and a small bird, mirrored in the right-hand one by a similar bird on a nest – the male and female poles of creation. 'The artist (is) older than the fish', reaching back to the 'fundamental slime of creation', wrote Lewis in 1919 (Lewis, 1919, p.65). In his smart suit, Eliot sits slightly hunched, avoiding our gaze. We are left to judge whether his respectability has been at the cost of turning his back on the sources of his creativity or whether they are still active in him. His haunted expression seems to chime with Eliot's own later belief that he had paid too high a price in personal happiness for being a poet.

SKETCH FOR HEAD OF T.S. ELIOT 1938

Charcoal on paper
315 x 263mm
(12³⁄8 x 10³⁄8in.)
Harry Ransom Center.
The University of Texas
at Austin

More vigorous than Lewis's earlier drawings of Eliot, this 'rough note' explores the structure of his head for the painting (p.69). Lewis also painted a preliminary oil sketch, the only occasion on which he is known to have done so. The sketch is now at Eliot House, Harvard University. The drawing has been signed by Eliot himself, perhaps as a sign of his alliance with Lewis in the public controversy that attended the finished portrait. Eliot wrote to Lewis that the portrait was 'one by which I am quite willing that posterity should know me, if it takes any interest in me at all.' (Letter from Eliot to Lewis, 21 April 1938, quoted in Lewis, 1963, p.251).

A NEW ZEITGEIST

PERSONALITIES OF THE 1930s

I AM THE MOST BROADMINDED 'LEFTWINGER' IN ENGLAND

For Wyndham Lewis the 1930s were something of a nightmare. He suffered repeated illness, requiring several operations on his bladder that nearly resulted in his death. Medical costs combined with frequent writs resulting in the suppression of books meant that he was chronically poor. Most important of all, his inveterately oppositional stance led him to take increasingly right-wing political positions during a period of left-wing orthodoxy. In 1931, two years before the Nazis came to power in Germany, Lewis wrote a sympathetic account of the German National Socialist movement (entitled *Hitler*), claiming that Hitler was a 'man of peace', that his economic policies would bring prosperity to Germany and that his racial views, though embarrassing, should not prevent the British public from seeing his merits. War became increasingly likely over time, and Lewis became more set in his views – and prepared to insinuate, though not to state, that a future war was being fomented by Jewish bankers in league with Soviet Russia. He wrote pro-appeasement books warning against the dangers of war, which he correctly believed would result in the dominance of Russia over central Europe. But when he revisited Berlin in late 1937 he changed his mind about the Nazis, and following the Munich Agreement in 1938 he wrote books attacking anti-Semitism and retracting his earlier views of Hitler.

Despite his unpopular political views, Lewis was on friendly terms with those he disagreed with. He remained a dual personality, capable of holding contradictory opinions simultaneously; capable of preferring Nationalist Spain yet donating a painting to raise funds for the Republic. This was what gave his art and imaginative writing such complexity. He was recognized, also, by members of a younger literary generation as one of the writers they could not afford to ignore. He is an important presence, for example, in the work of W.H. Auden (1907–73), and also influenced the cultural criticism of George Orwell (1903–50), who welcomed Lewis's 1938 study of Britishness, *The Mysterious Mr. Bull*, as a conversion to a left-wing outlook.[2]

Having concentrated on writing almost exclusively from 1926 to 1931, Lewis attempted in the 1930s to renew his career as a visual artist, beginning with an exhibition of portrait drawings, *Thirty Personalities*, in 1932 at London's Lefevre Gallery. His major effort, however, went into producing imaginative drawings and paintings (that show an influence from surrealism and de Chirico's 'metaphysical' painting) for an exhibition at the Leicester Galleries. He hoped to hold this in late 1933, but his recurrent illnesses meant that it did not materialize until 1937.

Portraiture, particularly in oils, also occupied him at this time. Lewis's line was now less 'inhuman' than it had been in the 1920s, and less powerful. His major novel of the period, *The Revenge for Love* (1937), also shows a humanity that the author of *The Wild Body* (1927) or *The Childermass* (1928) would have regarded as an aesthetic blemish. Lewis's greatest portraits of the 1930s are undoubtedly those of his fellow 'Men of 1914' and of his wife, Froanna, but others from the 1930s also show his continuing interest in human character.

Paul Edwards

NOTES

1 Lewis, 1937a, p.305.
2 Smith, 2007, pp.219–41; Munton, 2003.

G.K. CHESTERTON 1932

Pencil on paper
381 x 280mm
(15 x 11in.)
Harry Ransom Center.
The University
of Texas at Austin

G.K. Chesterton (1874–1936), now best known for his 'Father Brown' detective stories, was a novelist, editor and critic. Lewis had written an article, 'Futurism and the Flesh', defending visual abstraction against Chesterton's denunciation of its asceticism in the latter's *TP's Weekly* in July 1914 (Lewis, 1914a, pp.35–6). In this portrait Lewis emphasizes Chesterton's own fleshiness, which contrasts with an alert gaze behind the pince-nez. It was probably Chesterton's role as a Roman Catholic apologist that gave him a place in the *Thirty Personalities*. In *Time and Western Man* (1927), Lewis had discussed the theological implications of his own metaphysics, showing favour to Catholicism for the distance it keeps between the individual and God. Other Catholics in the portfolio included Augustus John's Jesuit son Henry and Martin D'Arcy. The latter reviewed *Time and Western Man* favourably and included a discussion of it in his study, *The Nature of Belief* (1931).

Wyndham Lewis. 1932.

WING-COMMANDER ORLEBAR
1932

Pencil and wash
on paper
320 x 279mm
(12⅝ x 11in.)
Leeds Museums
and Galleries (City
Art Gallery) UK/
The Bridgeman Art
Library

Wing-Commander (later Air Vice-Marshal) Augustus H. Orlebar (1897–1943) was a Schneider Trophy air ace, and the author of *Schneider Trophy: A Personal Account of High-Speed Flying and the Winning of the Schneider Trophy* (1933). His head reminded Lewis of Dante. The 'airman' as a heroic figure was frequently mythologized in writing of the 1930s, culminating in Rex Warner's deconstruction of the myth in his 1941 novel *The Aerodrome*. Jeffrey Meyers points out in his biography of Lewis that the portrait echoes Giovanni Bellini's (d.1516) portrait of Doge Leonardo Loredan in the National Gallery, London (Meyers, 1980, p.210). Orlebar's flying helmet is unfastened (like the bonnet of the Doge), but the dangling strap is given a characteristically Lewisian whiplash flourish. The airman is today's equivalent of the renaissance ruler, this portrait subtly suggests.

Wyndham Lewis. 1932.

REBECCA WEST 1932

Pencil on paper
430 x 310mm
(17 x 12¼in.)
National Portrait Gallery,
London (NPG 5693)

When this portrait was exhibited at the *Thirty Personalities* exhibition in 1932, Walter Sickert sent Lewis a telegram saying that it proved him to be 'the greatest portraitist of this or any other time' – rare praise from an artist who, though personally friendly, was not usually sympathetic to Lewis's art (quoted in Rothenstein, 1939, n.p.). The slight inconsistency in viewpoint applied to the two sides of the face (notably in eyes and chin) gives a sense of dynamism to the sitter's personality. Lewis met Rebecca West (1892–1983) in 1914 and published her short story, 'Indissoluble Matrimony', in *Blast*. She reviewed Lewis's first novel, *Tarr*, calling it 'a beautiful and serious work of art that reminds us of Dostoevsky only because it too is inquisitive about the soul, and because it contains one figure of vast moral significance which is worthy to stand beside Stavrogin' (quoted in Lewis, 1937a, p.93).

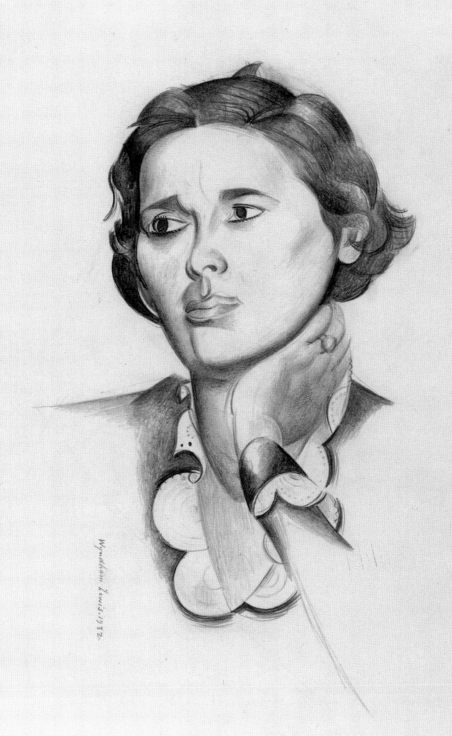

Wyndham Lewis. 1932.

NAOMI MITCHISON (THE TRAGIC MUSE)
1933

Pencil and wash
on paper
460 x 360mm
(18⅛ x 14⅛in.)
City Art Centre,
Edinburgh

Lewis met Naomi Mitchison (1897–1999) after she gave *The Apes of God* a favourable review, and they became close friends. She wrote for the feminist weekly, *Time and Tide*, to which Lewis himself became a frequent contributor. Married to Labour MP Dick Mitchison (1890–1970), she had firm left-wing and feminist views and did not take Lewis's anti-left-wing pronouncements altogether seriously. Her marriage was an 'open' one. She was sexually liberated, and later joked to an acquaintance that she would have sex with Lewis so that she did not have to listen to his opinions (personal communication: Jonathan Neale to author).

This drawing is one of a number Lewis produced of her wearing a Bulgarian dress with a stiffened front. Its alternative title seems to allude to Sir Joshua Reynolds's great portrait *Sarah Siddons as the Tragic Muse* (1783–4). Lewis may have noticed a similarity after producing the drawing, but Mitchison does seem to have been one of a few female sitters who were, effectively, his muses.

SPARTAN PORTRAIT (NAOMI MITCHISON) 1933

Pencil and
watercolour
on paper
390 x 267mm
(15³⁄₈ x 10¹⁄₂in.)
Wyndham Lewis
Memorial Trust:
G. and V. Lane
Collection

This severe, frontal pose with the sitter meeting the viewer's gaze face to face is unusual in Lewis's work, and is presumably the reason for the work's title. Naomi Mitchison made her name as a writer with her historical evocations of ancient Greece and Sparta, notably *Black Sparta* (1928). In 1935 Lewis and Mitchison worked together on a fantastical story, *Beyond This Limit*, for which he provided the illustrations. This collaboration took them both into a through-the-looking-glass world 'beyond this limit', inspiring some of Lewis's most whimsical inventions. Mitchison found that Lewis had the right kind of imagination to get on with her children (of whom he also produced portrait drawings). She was reported to have been shocked in later life when she read of his virtual abandonment of his own children.

NAOMI MITCHISON

1938

Oil on canvas
1016 x 762mm
(40 x 30in.)
Scottish National
Portrait Gallery.
Purchased with
assistance from
the Art Fund and
the Patrons of the
National Galleries
of Scotland 2003

Mitchison was writing *The Blood of the Martyrs* (1939) when this portrait was painted, and is depicted here occupied in her work. The small crucifixion scene to her right was specially designed for the portrait, while what looks like an elaborate monogram at the bottom left of the painting is actually an art deco ashtray. The cool colours once again emphasize a pensive severity in Mitchison's character, but she remains human and physically of this world (unlike *Praxitella*, p.13, for example), even if her imagination explores another. Lewis depicted this 'other' world in a 1938 painting, *Daydream of the Nubian*, in which a black woman, based on Mitchison, plucks a bubble from a stream on the bank of which she lies.

SIR STAFFORD CRIPPS 1934

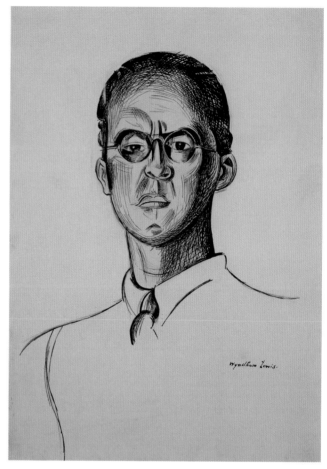

Pen and ink and
watercolour on paper
320 x 235mm
(12⅝ x 9¼in.)
Trustees of the Cecil
Higgins Art
Gallery, Bedford

Sir Stafford Cripps (1889–1952) became
most famous as the Chancellor of the
Exchequer who imposed 'austerity' on
the British people after the Second
World War. Cripps served as Solicitor-
General in Ramsay MacDonald's second
Labour Government, but refused to
serve in MacDonald's 1931 coalition,
associating himself with left-wing and
pacifist causes. He was a man of austere
Christian principles of self-denial and
service. Lewis produced this drawing as
one of a pair, reproduced in the *London
Mercury* in October 1934 under the title
'Two Dictators', the other being a now lost
portrait of Sir Oswald Mosley (catalogue
number 845 in Michel 1971). Mosley
himself noted the satirical edge to the
drawings, dubbing them 'the governess
and the gorilla' (O'Keeffe, 2000, p.346).

STEPHEN SPENDER
1938

Oil on canvas
1005 x 595mm
(39½ x 23½in.)
The Potteries
Museum and
Art Gallery,
Stoke-on-Trent

Lewis met Sir Stephen Spender (1909–95), who became one of the famous poets of the 1930s, in 1929 and planned to include some of his poems in a fourth issue of *The Enemy* that was never produced. Spender (probably mistakenly) believed he was the model for the childish anti-hero of *The Apes of God*, and later complained that Lewis's criticisms of Virginia Woolf were 'malicious'. Nevertheless, he organized the composition of a letter to *The Times* in 1937 during Lewis's large exhibition at the Leicester Galleries, praising his 'deep and original art' and urging that works from the show be acquired for the national collection. The twenty signatories included Henry Moore, W.H. Auden, Paul Nash, John Piper, Rebecca West and Naomi Mitchison. Lewis apparently wished to produce a series of portraits of poets, and approached Spender himself. The abstractions on the wall behind the sitter were invented for the occasion.

PORTRAIT OF A SMILING GENTLEMAN (LORD CARLOW)

1939

Oil on canvas
1016 x 711mm
(40 x 28in.)
Gift of Walter and
Harriet Michel.
The Herbert F. Johnson
Museum of Art,
Cornell University

George Viscount Carlow (1907–44) began collecting first editions and manuscripts of Lewis's books during the 1930s. (His collection is now held in the Rare Books Department of the Library of the State University of New York.) In 1938 Lewis wrote *The Role of Line in Art*, to be published by Carlow's small press, accompanied by reproductions of seven of his drawings. A 1941 air-raid destroyed the sheets and plates, but in 2007 the essay was published in a form close to the originally intended edition (Lewis, 1938a). This flattering and elegant portrait suggests that Lewis was at last capable of handling his patrons properly, providing them with what they paid for. It was an art he had failed to acquire in the 1920s – and which he promptly lost when he travelled to America in 1939, just before the outbreak of the Second World War.

JULIAN SYMONS 1939–49

Oil on canvas
735 x 635mm
(29 x 25in.)
Private Collection

Julian Symons (1912–94), younger brother of A.J.A. Symons (author of the 1934 *The Quest for Corvo*), published several essays about Lewis – placing him at the forefront of his judicious and entertaining study of modernism in literature (*Makers of the New*, 1987) and producing an anthology, *The Essential Wyndham Lewis* (1989). He also produced a Wyndham Lewis issue of the magazine *Twentieth Century Verse* (1937), which Lewis described as 'one of the milestones in my life as an artist' (quoted in O'Keeffe, 2000, p.373). The portrait was initiated at Lewis's suggestion and begun in 1939; Symons could only afford a £10 deposit. The first stage comprised several rapidly executed drawings in pen and ink. The portrait was abandoned during Lewis's stay in North America during the Second World War, but most of the work on the head was completed. The coffee table is also seen in the portrait of Ezra Pound, painted in 1939 (p.63); the abstraction behind Symons's head was again an invention.

FROANNA
PORTRAITS OF THE ARTIST'S WIFE

LIFE HAS BEEN SOMETHING OF A WAR FOR ME, AND THE WARRIORS – THE GAULS BEING AN EXCEPTION – HAVE USUALLY KEPT THE FIELD OF BATTLE FREE OF FEMALES

MAN'S DOMESTIC NATURE IS STRESSED HERE IN YOUR AMERICAN MATRIARCHY AND I HAVE FOUND MYSELF RATHER OVERSHADOWED BY MY WIFE, AS A MATTER OF FACT 1

Gladys Hoskins (1900–79) and Wyndham Lewis were married in October 1930. They had known each other since late 1918 and had lived together for some time. Gladys was the daughter of a gardener, thus from a far less privileged background than her husband. She was working in an aeroplane factory when she first met Lewis, at a party given by artist Gerald Brockhurst (1890–1978) to which she had been taken by an acquaintance who was an artist's model. Lewis's biographer reports that 'less is objectively known about this woman ... than about any other attachment of his life', and surmises that Gladys herself must have destroyed the documents and correspondence that would have contained biographical information.[2]

During the 1920s Gladys was a frequent model for Lewis's drawings and undoubtedly became his favourite. Lewis was capable of ruthless cruelty to his lovers, but somehow she managed to stay the course. She added a middle name, Anne, which led the German wife of Lewis's acquaintance Dr Meyrick Booth to call her 'Frau Anna' – hence the name Froanna. Most of Lewis's professional associates who have left memoirs of him in the 1930s report that they were dimly aware of Froanna's presence behind the scenes when they visited him at home, perhaps making the tea for them, and sometimes vaguely alluded to by Lewis himself. Privately, though, Lewis must have become dependent on her support during this period, when he underwent several major operations as the consequence of urinary tract infections, which left his health permanently affected.

Whether or not the experience of illness and of Froanna's care was the cause of the new humanity in Lewis's fiction and painting of the 1930s can only be a matter of speculation. The change is first evident in his 1934–5 novel *The Revenge for Love* (published in 1937), in which the experience of a character modelled on Froanna provides the novel's central meaning. Both the reader and, apparently, the narrator, care about Margot Stamp's fate, and this is something new in Lewis's fiction. A similar change takes place in Lewis's art. The 'human' – even the humane – had always seemed to him to provide too parochial a perspective for the criticism of life that art needed to effect. It is in the portrayals of Froanna in the 1930s that we see Lewis most content to recognize the humanity of another person. He produced seven paintings of her (besides portraying her many more times in works on paper) between 1936 and 1938.

In 1954, after becoming blind and after the nervous breakdown his new helplessness apparently triggered in Froanna, Lewis published another novel, *Self Condemned*, in which a figure based on Froanna is a major character. In one of its aspects this novel is a study of a marriage. The husband begins by regarding his wife as an embarrassment, her attractive physical attributes merely serving to advertise that his self-presentation as a pure intellectual is undermined by a common sexual appetite. He is forced to revalue this, as he becomes dependent on his wife's companionship during their bleak wartime exile in Canada. An underlying and persistent selfishness in him eventually brings about his wife's breakdown and suicide. In real life Froanna survived her husband by over twenty years, and was a great defender of his memory, always generous to visitors and scholars who visited her in Torquay to find out more about her remarkable husband.

Paul Edwards

NOTES

1 Letter to Mrs J. Rothenstein, December 1939, in Lewis, 1963, p.269.
2 O'Keeffe, 2000, p.248.

GIRL READING 1936

Pencil and wash
on paper
277 x 263mm
(10⅞ x 10⅜in.)
The British
Museum, London

This portrait is one of several drawings of Froanna produced in 1936 where she wears a blouse with full sleeves, exploited by Lewis for decorative visual interest. He always admired oriental art, especially that of the Sung period in China (960–1127), and its influence can often be traced in his work. In the 1930s, particularly in this series of drawings of his wife, the influence is clearer still. In earlier drawings, though the white of the support was often an integral part of the design, solid volumes were sharply delineated on it with incisive, controlling line. Now Lewis is happy to let elements of the form float and dissolve into the indefinite space of the white picture plane. The drawing is in no sense a sketch for a painting, but the series culminates in the painting, *Red Portrait* (p.96), in which Froanna wears the same full-sleeved blouse.

FROANNA (PORTRAIT OF THE ARTIST'S WIFE) 1937

Oil on canvas
760 x 635mm
(30 x 25in.)
Lent by Culture and
Sport Glasgow on
behalf of Glasgow
City Council

Froanna wears Lewis's red dressing gown in this portrait. In contrast to *Red Portrait* (p.96), this painting is a celebration of warm flesh and blood; we feel that viewing the picture gives us a direct encounter with a living person. The shape of the collar as it curves behind the sitter's neck is echoed at the left of the picture, behind her back, in the white outline of the dress that hangs over the back of her chair. Canadian critic and novelist Sheila Watson pointed out that within this outline the darker lines seem to suggest a helmeted head (Watson, 1967, p.5). Or perhaps it is a memento mori – a withered, skull-like face enshrouded by the white outlines of a cloak. It has been argued that Lewis's use of red in the two portraits of Froanna may be an aesthetic choice prompted by the beginning of a decline in his ability to see the colour as a result of damage to the optic nerves caused by the growth of his pituitary tumour (Conway, 1988).

RED PORTRAIT
1937

Oil on canvas
915 x 610mm
(36 x 24in.)
Wyndham Lewis
Memorial Trust:
G. and V. Lane
Collection

Lewis liked to paint worlds dominated by a single colour. Both this portrait, and the one on page 95, are dominated by red, though to very different effect. The dreamlike and insubstantial atmosphere is only partly created by the strange 'lunar' landscape above the mantelpiece. As in drawings leading up to the painting, the figure is an apparition that seems to emerge out of and dissolve into the ground on which it is minimally delineated.

The painting becomes a meditation on the transience of human identity as an organization of matter and its persistence as something that apparently transcends this material embodiment. Undoubtedly one of Lewis's greatest paintings, it completely contradicts the myth of Lewis the satirist and 'Enemy' – a myth he himself felt was necessary to his career. John Rothenstein wrote that Lewis said his objective in art was 'truth, beauty, the usual Platonic things' (Rothenstein, 1939, n.p.). Here such an ambition can be felt.

PENSIVE WOMAN
1938

Oil on canvas
594 x 445mm
(23⅜ x 17½in.)
Tullie House
Museum and Art
Gallery

The figure fills the canvas and dominates, with no visual or iconographic distraction from its surroundings. When Lewis painted himself in the early 1920s, he produced a variety of sometimes conflicting self-presentations. And with other sitters of the period he aimed for a purely visual truth.

This portrait shows, in a particularly striking manner, how his attention has shifted to a more psychological truth (conveyed, of course, by visual means). The painter is clearly interested above all in the internal life of the sitter. In fictional characters based loosely on Froanna, too (in *The Revenge for Love*, 1937, and *Self Condemned*, 1954), Lewis is concerned to explore their interior, psychological, life.

PORTRAIT OF THE ARTIST'S WIFE
1944

Pencil and coloured
chalks on blue paper
438 x 325mm
(17¼ x 12⅞in.)
The Trustees of the
Barber Institute
of Fine Arts, University
of Birmingham.
Acquired with generous
financial assistance
from the Art Fund and
the MLA/V&A
Purchase Grant

When Lewis and Froanna were in North
America, he produced several drawings of
their domestic life together in hotel rooms
and temporary apartments, including
still lifes of tea tables and depictions
of Froanna reading newspapers and
apparently brooding or depressed. The
present portrait dispenses with such
activities and accoutrements, but still
conveys an atmosphere of intensity and
strain. The intertwined hands (a frequent
motif in Lewis's portrait drawings) help
convey this nervous intensity, but it
is mostly achieved by the minimally
delineated eyes with their fixed pupils.
The decorativeness of the elaborate
turban-style headdress is in disturbing
contrast with the naked gaze of the sitter.
Lewis bought his blue paper at a drugstore,
and it was possibly the paper that led him
to turn to coloured chalks and pastels as
a medium at this time.

[98]

THE SEA-MISTS OF THE WINTER

NORTH AMERICA AND BLINDNESS

ALTHOUGH
I HAVE
SUCCEEDED
IN MAKING
A LIVING
OF SORTS
HERE IN CANADA
— MOSTLY BY
PORTRAIT-PAINTING

— IT IS VERY
GRUESOME WORK
STRUGGLING WITH
PEOPLE ABOUT
THE SHAPES OF
THEIR NOSES AND
THE SIZE OF
THEIR FEET [1]

On 2 September 1939 Lewis and his wife sailed on the *Empress of Britain* for Quebec. They were not to return to London for six years, spending the duration of the Second World War in Canada and the United States of America. Lewis had planned a trip to North America some time in advance, hoping to reap a rich reward as a portraitist there. He told Julian Symons that he had no wish to remain in Europe while it tore itself apart a second time, and in peacetime England he had barely managed to earn enough to remain solvent. America, he thought, was where his best prospects lay. His father was American, and Lewis had made several visits there himself. This would be a chance for him to explore his American roots around Buffalo, upstate New York and Canada. In fact, the long sojourn in America was something of a nightmare for him – though Froanna enjoyed taking a more public part in his social-cum-business life. Lewis seems to have expected to be treated as an important writer and painter, and to be able to continue his two careers with little trouble. In England, his 'Enemy' strategy of consistently taking a line that contradicted the views of the liberal cultural elite did not lead to total neglect and ostracism; but in North America he found it much more difficult to secure a foothold and achieve economic security. The insecurity seems to have led to a reversion to his personality of the 1920s. When he found patrons and friends who tried to help him or lent money, he would quarrel with them or otherwise alienate them.

Commissioned portraits, teaching contracts and private patronage were sufficient to enable the Lewises to survive, however. Their sufferings (which Lewis knew were nothing compared to those of the real victims of the war) led him to a profound revaluation of some of his most firmly held attitudes – first, in a series of fantastic watercolours produced in Toronto during a long sojourn in the Tudor Hotel (November 1940 to May 1943). The abstractions that he had produced for the backgrounds of the portraits of Eliot, Mitchison, Spender and others – of brooding bird forms, the crucifixion, landscape and creation – now occupied the foreground of his art, while portraiture became little more than an economic activity. His commissioned portraits, with a few exceptions, are competent (sometimes not even that) and uninspired. His most successful portraiture is more domestic, of Froanna or of personal friends. His literary revaluation occurred in the novel based on the stay in the Tudor Hotel, *Self Condemned*. In *America and Cosmic Man* (1948) he completed the revolution in his political outlook that had begun in 1937. This study of political history embraces the rootless democracy of America as a model for an internationalist politics. 'The earth has become one big village',[2] he wrote, in a sentence that inspired Marshall McLuhan (a disciple and helper of Lewis during the war) to develop his concept of the 'Global Village'.

Lewis noticed a marked deterioration in his sight in the summer of 1941. It continued deteriorating more rapidly towards the end of the decade after his return to England, and was caused by a pituitary tumour pressing on, and gradually destroying, the optic nerve. In 1951, in a moving article for *The Listener*, 'The Sea-Mists of the Winter', Lewis announced that he would have to give up his work as the magazine's art critic as he could no longer see a picture. His own painting had virtually ceased in 1949, with the late portrait of T.S. Eliot being his last important work (p.107). He anticipated total blindness: 'Pushed into an unlighted room, the door banged and locked for ever, I shall then have to light a lamp of aggressive voltage in my mind to keep at bay the night'.[3] Although painting was at an end for him, he wrote seven more books, all in longhand on paper that remained obstinately blank for him, before his death from kidney failure and the effects of the tumour in March 1957. In July 1956, frail and blind, Lewis had attended the private view of *Wyndham Lewis and Vorticism*, the retrospective exhibition of his work organized by Sir John Rothenstein at the Tate, where he was honoured by friends and former 'enemies'.

Paul Edwards

NOTES

1 Letter to Archibald McLeish,
   21 October 1941 (Lewis, 1963, p.302).
2 Lewis, 1948, p.16.
3 Lewis, 1951, p.765.

CHANCELLOR SAMUEL CAPEN
1939

Oil on canvas
1930 x 890mm
(76 x 35in.)
The Poetry
Collection of the
University Libraries,
State University of
New York at Buffalo

This portrait of Samuel Capen, Chancellor of the State University of New York, was not the passport to success that Lewis hoped for. He was 'trying to make it as academic as possible and still keep it a work of art' (O'Keeffe, 2000, p.405). But he alienated one faction of Buffalo's cultural elite by refusing to exhibit it at the Albright Art Gallery (now the Albright-Knox). His unease may have been because it was his only 'official' public portrait commission.

He struggled to finish it, and by some accounts tried to hand it over when there was still work to be done. The cubist landscape, tablecloth and books, including Lewis's 1939 collected writings on art (Lewis 1939b), with a reproduction of his 1938 portrait of T.S. Eliot (p.69) on the dust jacket – not visible here – are late additions. The Capen portrait may not be in the same class as the Eliot portrait, but the lean, ascetic El Greco-ish elongation of the figure and head is very effective.

MALCOLM MACDONALD
1945

Coloured chalk
on paper
365 x 273mm
(14³/₈ x 10³/₄in.)
National Portrait Gallery,
London (NPG 5739)

Malcolm MacDonald (1901–81), son of
Ramsay MacDonald, was British High
Commissioner of Canada from 1941
to 1946. He was involved in tortuous
negotiations to extricate a completed
painting from Lewis, commissioned to
represent Canada's war effort. MacDonald
was interested in Lewis's plans for *America
and Cosmic Man*, corresponding with
him concerning Canadian culture and
painting (which Lewis admired, despite his
frustration with Canada), and helped Lewis
with $150 for his fare back to England in
1945. The portrait may have been part
of this arrangement. Like many whom
Lewis imposed upon, MacDonald seems
to have regarded him with esteem, and
the portrait shows sympathetic insight on
Lewis's part. He always took great trouble
over depicting his sitters' mouths, leaving
here preliminary sketches at the bottom
of the sheet. The signature alongside them
suggests that Lewis considered them an
integral part of the completed work.

STUDY FOR PORTRAIT OF T.S. ELIOT
1949

Coloured chalk
on paper
542 x 320mm
(21¾ x 12⅝in.)
Jenny Page

In his article 'The Sea-Mists of the Winter', Lewis described the effect of his declining sight on his painting. When painting Eliot in 1949, he wrote, he had to 'draw up very closely to the sitter to see exactly how the hair sprouted out of the forehead, and how the curl of the nostril wound up into the dark interior of the nose' (Lewis 1950a). The sketch is remarkably assured and integrated compared with another that exists of the whole seated figure, where Lewis clearly had difficulty in describing the articulation of the limbs (not catalogued in Michel; currently at the Harry Ransom Humanities Research Center Art Collection, University of Texas at Austin). The present work arguably offers a more impressive insight into the sitter than the head in the final painting (p.107).

T.S. ELIOT
1949

Oil on canvas
865 x 555mm
(34 x 21⁷/₈in.)
The Master
and Fellows,
Magdalene College,
Cambridge

This was probably Lewis's last completed oil before he went blind. Although Lewis said in interview that he wished to paint a portrait of a man haunted by a vision ('White Fire', *Time* (Atlantic Overseas Edition), 30 May 1949, p.32), the sitter appears considerably less haunted than in 1938 (which may simply be due to Lewis's failing sight). The overall design and disposition of the foreshortened figure, however, show no failing in Lewis's compositional powers. This last portrait of one of the 20th century's greatest creators, by another of the century's greatest creators – commemorating a literary relationship of over thirty years – has a significance beyond any consideration of its value as a painting. Lewis offered it to the Tate for £250, but it was rejected. As honorary fellow of Magdalene College, Eliot was required to pay for a portrait – the college was assured that the portrait was not a puzzling cubist affair, and Eliot paid Lewis £300 for it (O'Keeffe, 2000, pp.545–6).

FURTHER READING

CONWAY, 1988
J.F. Conway, 'An Early Effect of Wyndham Lewis's Pituitary Tumour on his Art: An Inquiry Prompted by a note in *The World through Blunted Sight*', *Eye*, no. 2, pp.677–81

CORBETT, 1998
D. P. Corbett, '"Grief with a Yard Wide Grin": War and Wyndham Lewis's Tyros', *Wyndham Lewis and the Art of Modern War*, ed. D.P. Corbett (Cambridge University Press), pp.99–123

EDWARDS, 2000a
P. Edwards, *Wyndham Lewis: Painter and Writer* (Yale University Press, New Haven and London)

EDWARDS, 2000b
P. Edwards (ed.), *Blast: Vorticism, 1914–1918* (Ashgate, Aldershot)

ELIOT, 1988
T.S. Eliot, *The Letters of T.S. Eliot, Vol. 1: 1898–1922*, ed. V. Eliot (Faber, London)

FARRINGTON, 1980
J. Farrington, *Wyndham Lewis* (Lund Humphries, London with Manchester City Art Galleries)

GASIOREK, 2003
A. Gasiorek, *Wyndham Lewis and Modernism* (Northcote House, Tavistock)

HUMPHREYS, 1985
R. Humphreys, 'Demon Pantechnicon Driver: Pound in the London Vortex, 1908–1920', *Pound's Artists: Ezra Pound and the Visual Arts in London, Paris and Italy* (Tate Gallery, London), pp.33–80

HUMPHREYS, 2004
R. Humphreys, *Wyndham Lewis* (Tate Publishing, London)

LEWIS, 1914a
W. Lewis, 'Futurism and the Flesh', *Creatures of Habit and Creatures of Change: Essays on Art, Literature and Society 1914–1956*, ed. P. Edwards (reprinted, Black Sparrow Press, Santa Rosa, 1989)

LEWIS, 1914b
W. Lewis (ed.), *Blast*, no. 1 (July)

LEWIS, 1915
W. Lewis (ed.), *Blast*, no. 2 (July)

LEWIS, 1917
W. Lewis, 'Imaginary Letters: The Code of a Herdsman', *The Little Review*, vol. 4, no. 7 (July), pp.3–7

LEWIS, 1918
W. Lewis, *Tarr: The 1918 Version*, ed. P. O'Keeffe (reprinted, Black Sparrow Press, 1990)

LEWIS, 1919
W. Lewis, *The Caliph's Design: Architects! Where is Your Vortex?*, ed. P. Edwards, (reprinted, Black Sparrow Press, 1986)

LEWIS, 1921
W. Lewis (ed.), *The Tyro*, no. 1 (April)

LEWIS, 1922a
W. Lewis, 'The Credentials of the Painter', *Creatures of Habit and Creatures of Change: Essays on Art, Literature and Society 1914–1956*, ed. P. Edwards (reprinted, Black Sparrow Press, 1989), pp.66–76

LEWIS, 1922b
W. Lewis (ed.), *The Tyro*, no. 2 (March)

LEWIS, 1926
W. Lewis, *The Art of Being Ruled*, ed. R.W. Dasenbrock (reprinted, Black Sparrow Press, 1989)

LEWIS, 1927a
W. Lewis (ed.), *The Enemy*, no. 1 (January)

LEWIS, 1927b
W. Lewis, *Time and Western Man*, ed. P. Edwards (reprinted, Black Sparrow Press,

LEWIS 1927c
W. Lewis (ed.), *The Enemy*, no. 2 (September)

LEWIS, 1927d
W. Lewis, *The Lion and the Fox: The Rôle of the Hero in the Plays of Shakespeare* (Richards Press, London)

LEWIS, 1929a
W. Lewis (ed.), *The Enemy*, no. 3 (March)

LEWIS, 1929b
W. Lewis, 'A World Art and Tradition', *Wyndham Lewis on Art: Collected Writings 1913–1956*, eds W. Michel and C.J. Fox (reprinted, Thames and Hudson, London, 1969), pp.255–9

LEWIS, 1930
W. Lewis, *The Apes of God* (The Arthur Press, London)

LEWIS, 1931
W. Lewis, *Hitler* (Chatto and Windus, London)

LEWIS, 1932
W. Lewis, *Thirty Personalities and a Self Portrait* (Desmond Harmsworth, London)

LEWIS, 1934
W. Lewis, *Men Without Art* (Cassell, London)

LEWIS, 1935
W. Lewis, 'Beginning', *Creatures of Habit and Creatures of Change: Essays on Art, Literature and Society 1914–1956*, ed. P. Edwards (reprinted, Black Sparrow Press, 1989), pp.262–7

FURTHER READING

LEWIS, 1937a
W. Lewis, *Blasting and Bombardiering* (Eyre and Spottiswoode, London)

LEWIS, 1937b
W. Lewis, *The Revenge for Love* (reprinted, Penguin, London, 2004)

LEWIS, 1937c
W. Lewis, *Count your Dead: They are Alive! Or, A New War in the Making* (Lovat Dickson, London)

LEWIS, 1938a
W. Lewis, *The Role of Line in Art*, ed. P.W. Nash (reprinted, The Strawberry Leaf Press, Witney, 2007)

LEWIS, 1938b
W. Lewis, *The Mysterious Mr. Bull* (Robert Hale, London)

LEWIS, 1938c
W. Lewis, 'Fifty Years of Painting', reprinted, *Apollo*, vol. xci, no. 97 (March 1970), pp.218–23

LEWIS, 1939a
W. Lewis, 'Super-Nature versus Super-Real', *Wyndham Lewis on Art: Collected Writings 1913–1956*, eds W. Michel and C.J. Fox (reprinted, Thames and Hudson, London, 1969), pp.303–33

LEWIS, 1939b
W. Lewis, *Wyndham Lewis the Artist: From Blast to Burlington House* (Laidlaw & Laidlaw, London)

LEWIS, 1939c
W. Lewis, *The Hitler Cult, and How it will End* (Dent, London)

LEWIS, 1948
W. Lewis, *America and Cosmic Man* (Nicolson and Watson, London)

LEWIS, 1950a
W. Lewis, 'Ezra Pound', *Ezra Pound: Collection of Essays...*, ed. P. Russell (Peter Nevill, London)

LEWIS, 1950b
W. Lewis, 'Royal Academy', *Creatures of Habit and Creatures of Change: Essays on Art, Literature and Society 1914–1956*, ed. P. Edwards (reprinted, Black Sparrow Press, 1989), pp.355–9

LEWIS, 1950c
W. Lewis, *Rude Assignment: A Narrative of my Career up-to-date* (Hutchinson, London)

LEWIS, 1951
W. Lewis, 'The Sea-Mists of the Winter', *The Listener*, vol. xlv, no. 1158 (10 May), p.765

LEWIS, 1954
W. Lewis, *Self Condemned*, ed. R. Smith (reprinted, Black Sparrow Press, 1983)

LEWIS, 1956
W. Lewis, 'Introduction', *Wyndham Lewis and Vorticism* (Tate Gallery, London), pp.3–4

LEWIS, 1963
W. Lewis, *The Letters of Wyndham Lewis*, ed. W.K. Rose (Methuen, London)

LEWIS, 1973
W. Lewis, *The Roaring Queen* (Secker and Warburg, London)

MASTIN, 1992
C. Mastin, Robert Stacey and Thomas Dilworth, *"The Talented Intruder": Wyndham Lewis in Canada, 1939–1945* (Art Gallery of Windsor, Windsor, Ontario)

MATERER, 1985
T. Materer (ed.), *Pound/Lewis: The Letters of Ezra Pound and Wyndham Lewis* (New Directions, New York)

MEYERS, 1980
J. Meyers, *The Enemy: A Biography of Wyndham Lewis* (Routledge and Kegan Paul, London)

MICHEL, 1971
W. Michel, *Wyndham Lewis: Paintings and Drawings* (Thames and Hudson, London)

MUNTON, 2003
A. Munton, 'George Orwell, Wyndham Lewis and the Origins of Cultural Studies' (accessed 18 December 2007), http://www.arasite.org/amlewis.html

NORMAND, 1987
T. Normand, 'The Intoxication of Death', *Enemy News*, no. 24 (Summer), pp.10–16

O'KEEFFE, 2000
P. O'Keeffe, *Some Sort of Genius: A Life of Wyndham Lewis*, (Jonathan Cape, London)

ROTHENSTEIN, 1939
J. Rothenstein, 'Great British Masters – 26: Wyndham Lewis', *Picture Post* (25 March)

SMITH, 2007
S. Smith, 'Broadminded Leftwingers and Marxian Playboys: Wyndham Lewis, W.H. Auden and the Literary Left in the 1930s', *Wyndham Lewis the Radical: Essays on Literature and Modernity*, ed. C. Cunchillos Jaime (Peter Lang, Bern), pp.219–41

WATSON, 1967
S. Watson, 'The Great War, Wyndham Lewis and the Underground Press', *ArtsCanada*, no. 114 (November), pp.3–17

ILLUSTRATION LIST

Media, dimensions, locations and lenders are given in the captions. Further acknowledgments, details of comparative images and reference numbers from Walter Michel's 1971 catalogue raisonné (where relevant) are given below.

Page 13
Praxitella, 1920–1. Michel P30. Image © Leeds City Galleries.

Page 14 (left)
Portrait of the Artist as the Painter Raphael, 1921. Michel P28 and P29. Image © Manchester City Galleries.

Page 14 (right)
William Shakespeare by Martin Droeshout, 1623 or 1663–4. Image © National Portrait Gallery, London (NPG 185).

Page 21
Self-portrait, 1911. Michel 26. Image © C.J. Fox.

Page 23
Self-portrait, 1920. Michel 423. Image © Private Collection.

Page 25
Mr Wyndham Lewis as a Tyro, 1920–1. Michel P27. Image © Ferens Art Gallery, Hull City Museums and Art Gallery.

Page 26
Portrait of the Artist as the Painter Raphael, 1921. Michel P28 and P29. Image © Manchester City Galleries.

Page 27
Self-portrait with Hat, 1930. Michel 703. Image © Private Collection.

Page 28
Self-portrait with Hat, 1932. Michel 782. National Portrait Gallery, London (NPG 4528).

Page 29
Self-portrait, 1932. Michel 781. Image © Private Collection.

Page 30
Self-portrait with Pipe, 1938. Michel 922. Image © The Poetry Collection of the University Libraries, State University of New York at Buffalo.

Page 35
L'Ingénue, 1919. Michel 334. Image © Manchester City Galleries.

Page 36
Woman Knitting, 1920. Michel 440. Image © Manchester City Galleries.

Page 37
Study for Painting (Seated Lady), 1920. Michel 433. Image © Manchester City Galleries.

Page 38
Mary Webb (Girl Looking Down), 1919. Michel 329 Private Collection.

Page 39
Edward Wadsworth, 1920. Michel 436. Image © and on loan with kind permission from the Junior Common Room Art Collection of Pembroke College, Oxford.

Page 41
Edith Sitwell, 1921. Michel 488. Image © Trustees of the Cecil Higgins Art Gallery, Bedford, England.

Page 42
Edith Sitwell, 1921. Michel 485. Image © National Portrait Gallery, London (NPG 4464).

Page 43
Edith Sitwell, 1923–35. Michel P36. Image © Tate. Presented by Sir Edward Beddington-Behrens 1943.

Page 44
Edith Sitwell, 1923. Michel 592. Image © National Portrait Gallery, London (NPG 4465).

Page 45
Virginia Woolf, 1921. Michel 500. Image © Victoria & Albert Museum.

Page 47
Edwin Evans, 1922. Michel P35. Image © National Galleries of Scotland.

Page 48
Mrs Workman, 1923. Michel 599. Image © Private Collection.

Page 49
Nancy Cunard, 1922. Michel 524. Image © British Council.

Page 51
Mrs Schiff, 1923–4. Michel P37. Image © Tate. Purchased 1956.

Page 52
Sacheverell Sitwell, 1922. Michel 554. Image © Private Collection.

Page 56
Ezra Pound, 1919. Not catalogued in Michel. Image © Harry Ransom Center, The University of Texas at Austin.

Page 57
Ezra Pound, 1920. Michel 412. Image © National Portrait Gallery, London (NPG 6728).

Page 59
Ezra Pound, 1921. Michel 473. Image © Private Collection.

Page 61
Ezra Pound, 1938. Michel 919. Image © Private Collection.

ILLUSTRATION LIST

Page 63
Ezra Pound, 1939. Michel P99.
Image © Tate. Purchased 1939.

Page 64
James Joyce, 1920. Not catalogued
in Michel. Image © Private Collection.

Page 65
James Joyce, 1921. Michel 463. Image
© National Gallery of Ireland, Dublin.
Photo © National Gallery of Ireland.

Page 66
James Joyce, 1921. Michel 397. Image
© Sheffield Galleries and Museums Trust.

Page 67
T.S. Eliot, 1925. Not catalogued in Michel.
Image © Harry Ransom Center,
The University of Texas at Austin.

Page 69
T.S. Eliot, 1938. Michel P80. Image
© Durban Municipal Art Gallery.

Page 70
Sketch for Head of T.S. Eliot, 1938.
Not catalogued in Michel. Image
© Harry Ransom Center, The University
of Texas at Austin.

Page 75
G.K. Chesterton, 1932. Michel 738.
Image © Harry Ransom Center,
The University of Texas at Austin.

Page 77
Wing-Commander Orlebar, 1932.
Michel 776. Image © Leeds Museums
and Galleries (City Art Gallery) UK/
The Bridgeman Art Library.

Page 79
Rebecca West, 1932. Michel 786. Image
© National Portrait Gallery, London
(NPG 5693).

Page 80
Naomi Mitchison (The Tragic Muse),
1933. Michel 952. Image © City Art
Centre, Edinburgh.

Page 81
Spartan Portrait (Naomi Mitchison), 1933.
Michel 809. Image © Wyndham Lewis
Memorial Trust: G. and V. Lane Collection.

Page 83
Naomi Mitchison, 1938. Michel P96.
Image © Scottish National Portrait Gallery.
Purchased with the assistance from the
Art Fund and the Patrons of the National
Galleries of Scotland 2003.

Page 84
Sir Stafford Cripps, 1934. Michel 842.
Image © Trustees of the Cecil Higgins
Art Gallery, Bedford, England.

Page 85
Stephen Spender, 1938. Michel P86.
Image © The Potteries Museum and
Art Gallery, Stoke-on-Trent.

Page 87
*Portrait of a Smiling Gentleman
(Lord Carlow)*, 1939. Michel P98.
Gift of Walter and Harriet Michel.
Photography courtesy and © of the
Herbert F. Johnson Museum of Art,
Cornell University.

Page 88
Julian Symons, 1939–49. Michel
P127. Image © Private Collection.

Page 93
Girl Reading, 1936. Michel 858.
Image © The British Museum,
London.

Page 95
Froanna (Portrait of the Artist's Wife),
1937. Michel P71. Image © Culture and
Sport Glasgow (Museums). Lent by
Culture and Sport Glasgow on behalf
of Glasgow City Council.

Page 96
Red Portrait, 1937. Michel P76.
Image © Wyndham Lewis Memorial
Trust: G. and V. Lane Collection.

Page 97
Pensive Woman, 1938. Michel P 85.
Image © Tullie House Museum and
Art Gallery.

Page 98
Portrait of the Artist's Wife, 1944.
Michel 958. Image © Trustees of
the Barber Institute of Fine Arts,
University of Birmingham. Acquired
with generous financial assistance
from the Art Fund and the MLA/V&A
Purchase Grant.

Page 102
Chancellor Samuel Capen, 1939.
Michel P94. Image © The Poetry
Collection of the University Libraries,
State University of New York at Buffalo.

Page 103
Malcolm MacDonald, 1945.
Michel 1072. Image © National
Portrait Gallery, London (NPG 5739).

Page 105
Study for Portrait of T.S. Eliot, 1949.
Michel 1095. Image © Jenny Page.

Page 107
T.S. Eliot, 1949. Michel P124.
Image © The Master and Fellows,
Magdalene College, Cambridge.

INDEX